The Archbishop Who Killed a Man
and other Anecdotes from Christian History

Other books by Dan Graves

Scientists of Faith; 48 Biographies of Historic Scientists and Their Christian Faith. Kregel, 1996

Doctors Who Followed Christ; 32 Biographies of Eminent Physicians and Their Christian Faith. Kregel, 1999.

The Earth Will Reel from its Place; Scientific Confirmation for Bible Prophecies of Geological Upheaval. Authorhouse, 2006.

With Ken Curtis

Great Women in Christian History; 37 women who changed their world. Christian History Institute, 2004.

This Day in Christian History; 366 Compelling Events in the History of the Church. Christian History Institute, 2005.

Adaptations

From Christ to Luther (in preparation).

Cover Design, Book Layout, and Edits

Maxims of Wisdom from the Writings of the Devout by Gene Graves. Lulu Press, 2007.

The Archbishop Who Killed a Man
and other Anecdotes from Christian History

Amusing Acts and Events, Curiosities, Gallantries,
Last Words, Profound Truths, and Witticisms.

Compiled and edited by Dan Graves.

Trustworthy Publications, 2008
www.trustworthypublications.com

Copyright © 2008 by
Trustworthy Publications

All rights reserved.
First edition, 2008.
Design by Dan Graves.

ISBN: 978-0-6152-1629-4

For Ken Curtis, whose idea this was and who made it possible.

Faith makes, life proves, trials confirm, and death crowns the Christian.
— Johann Georg Christian Hopfner

Abbot, George (1562-1633). The Archbishop Who Killed a Man.

Although George Abbot was not the most eminent man of faith in England, James I selected him in 1611 to be Archbishop of Canterbury because he had been useful to the king in Scotland. Abbot had served on the committee which prepared the translation of the Bible known as the Authorized or King James Version. Although he had been a vocal Puritan, he accepted the Church of England organization and persecuted nonconformists with the cruelty typical of the times. An accident in 1621 cast a shadow over his remaining life.

IN THE SUMMER OF 1621 the archbishop made a tour through Hampshire for the benefit of his health, and was invited by Lord Zouche to shoot on his estate. On July 24, while hunting deer in the park, he released an arrow from a cross-bow which accidentally struck Peter Hawkins, one of Lord Zouche's keepers, who had been warned to keep out of the way. The arrow pierced his right arm, severing an artery, and the unfortunate man bled to death in an hour.

Though the archbishop was in no way to blame, this accident threw him into deep melancholy. He immediately bestowed an annuity of £20 upon the widow, which soon procured her another husband. For the rest of his life Abbot observed a monthly fast on Tuesday, the day of the fatal occurrence.

The incident caused much talk, and the question arose whether the archbishop, by having blood on his hands, had not become disqualified to discharge the duties of his office. In contrast to the cruelty of some of Abbot's opponents, King James showed much kindness. On hearing of the accident, he remarked: "An angel might have miscarried in this way."

Four bishops, one of who was Abbot's old enemy, Laud, Bishop-elect of St. David's, were at that time waiting to be consecrated, and three of them refused to receive the rite from Abbot, "lest they might be attainted with the contagion of his scandal and uncanonical condition." The king appointed commissioners to make full inquiry into the law of the case. They eventually agreed that the archbishop might receive restitution by the king. James accordingly commissioned eight bishops under the Great Seal to acquit Abbott of all irregularity and pronounce him capable of the full authority of a primate.

The incident cast a shadow over the remainder of the archbishop's career. Shortly before his death, when he was on his way to Croydon, his coach stopped for a crowd of women gathered in the road. On his complaining of the delay some of them shouted, "You had best shoot an arrow at us."

- Adapted from A. E. McKilliam's *A Chronicle of the Archbishops of Canterbury*. London: James Clarke & Co., 1913.

Alexander, Archibald (1772-1851). How to Handle Doubt.

Archibald Alexander was the first theological professor of Princeton. He proved an able educator, a man of deep faith, and a highly regarded author. Here is his counsel to a man who doubted his salvation.

A STUDENT ONCE CALLED on Archibald Alexander in great distress of mind, doubting whether he had been converted.

Alexander encouraged him to open his heart to him. After he was through, he laid his hand on his head, saying, "My young brother, you know what repentance is—what faith in Christ is. You think you once repented and once believed. Now don't fight your doubts; go it all over again. Repent now; believe in Christ—that's the way to have a consciousness of acceptance with God. I have to do both very often. Go to your room and give yourself to Christ this very moment, and let doubts go. If you have not been his disciple, be one now. Don't fight the devil on his own ground. Choose the ground of Christ's righteousness and atonement and then fight him."

• Adapted from Walter Baxendale's *Dictionary of Anecdote, Incident, Illustrative Fact*. New York: Thomas Whittaker, 1889.

Alfred the Great (849-899). Alfred Enlists Asser.

No king of England had a higher character than Alfred—a true Christian. He was always recruiting learned and pious men to educate his people. One such was the Welsh monk Asser, who became his biographer. Alfred pressed him to join his service.

I REPLIED THAT I could not without thought, and rashly, promise such things, for it seemed to me wrong to leave those sacred places where I had been bred and educated, and had received the tonsure and ordination, for the sake of any earthly honor or promotion. Upon this he said, 'If you cannot altogether yield to my request, at least let me have your service in part; spend six months of the year with me, and the other six in Wales.'

I answered that I could not even promise this hastily, without the advice of my friends. But at length, when I saw that he was very anxious for my service (though I know not why), I promised that if my life were spared I would come back in six months with such a reply as would be welcome to him, as well as advantageous to me and my friends. With this answer he was content, and when I had given him a pledge to return at the appointed time, on the fourth day I left him, and returned on horseback toward my own country.

After my departure I was stricken by a violent fever at Winchester, where I lay for a year and a week, night and day, without hope of recovery. At the appointed time, therefore, I could not redeem my pledge of returning to him, and he sent messengers to speed my journey and ask the cause of the delay. As I was unable to ride to him I sent a messenger to tell him the cause of the delay and to assure him that if I recovered I would fulfill what I had promised. So when my sickness left me, by the advice of all my friends, for the benefit of our holy place and of all who dwelt therein, I did as I had promised the King, and devoted myself to his service on condition that I should remain with him six months in every year, either continuously, or alternately—three months in Wales, and three in England."

- Asser. "Life of Alfred," adapted from Thomas Hughes' *Alfred the Great*. New York: Perkins Book Co., [1902] .

Ancillon, David (1617-1692). Loss of a Noble Library.

David Ancillon was a pastor of the Reformed Church in Metz and author of a life of the reformer William Farel.

FROM HIS EARLIEST YEARS David Ancillon's devotion to study was so great as to require the interposition of his father, to prevent his health being seriously affected by it; he was described as "intemperately studious." The Jesuits of Metz gave him the free range of their college library; but his studies led him to Protestantism, and in 1633 he moved to Geneva, and devoted himself to the duties of the Reformed Church. Throughout an honorable life his love of books never diminished; and having a fortune by marriage, he gratified himself in constantly collecting them, so that he ultimately possessed one of the finest private libraries in France. For very many years his life passed peaceably and happily amid his books and his duties, until the revocation of the Edict of Nantes drove him from his country. His noble library was scattered at waste-paper prices; "thus in a single day was destroyed the labor, care, and expense of 44 years." He died seven years later at Brandenburg.

- Adapted from Isaac D'Israeli's *Curiosities of Literature.* London: Frederick and Warne, 1881.

Annan, Robert (Nineteenth Century). Eternity; Entering Heaven.

Robert Annan was a prodigal, who upon his conversion became a soul-winner and a helper of the poor.

Eternity. ROBERT ANNAN of Dundee, Scotland, was one of the worst men who ever lived in that town, but after his conversion became one of its most useful soul-winners. On leaving his cottage one morning to go to his mission work, he took a piece of chalk from his pocket and wrote on the flagstone of the walk which led to his house the single word "Eternity."

A few minutes later he saw a child fall from a ship. Being a bold swimmer, he threw off his coat and shoes and plunged into the bay. He saved the child, but at the cost of his own life. His body was carried home over the word "Eternity" which he had written a few hours before. The Earl of Aberdeen caused it to be cut into the stone as a permanent memorial and thousands came to see it.

- Adapted from Ira D. Sankey's *My Life and the Story of the Gospel Hymns.* Philadelphia: Sunday School Times, 1907.

Entering Heaven. DISCUSSION TURNED TO HEAVEN and someone said to Robert, "I'll be satisfied if I manage somehow to get in."

"What!" exclaimed Robert, pointing to a sunken ship that had just been dragged up the Tay. "Would you like to be pulled into heaven by two tugs, like the *London* over there? I tell you I would like to go in with all my sails set and colors flying."

- Adapted from Walter Baxendale's *Dictionary of Anecdote, Incident, Illustrative Fact.* New York: Thomas Whittaker, 1889.

Alphege (954-1012). Death for Compassion.

Alphege, the Archbishop of Canterbury from 1006 to 1012, became a martyr and saint through his selflessness.

ALPHEGE HAD been Archbishop of Canterbury just six years when Danish raiders took him captive in 1011 and demanded an enormous ransom. Knowing that the Saxons had already been bled dry by such demands and could not pay without serious suffering, Alphege refused to seek the payment.

At a drunken feast on April 19, 1012, the Danes repeated their demand. Alphege again refused. The raiders pelted him with bones, stones and other hard objects, although their leader, Thorkell the Tall, pleaded for the bishop's life, offering in exchange for it everything he owned except his boat. He was ignored, and a Dane named Thurm smacked Alphege in the head with his axe. Other Danes finished him off with a beating. The Saxons buried him with honors and recognized him as a martyr and saint.

- This information appears in most accounts of the saint's life.

Aquinas, Thomas (ca. 1225-1274). Discerns True Value; Wrecks a Frightening Invention.

Thomas Aquinas was the most notable Christian philosopher of the thirteenth century, on whose system, called Thomism, much Catholic theology is based to this day.

True value. THOMAS AQUINAS, nicknamed "the Angelic Doctor," was highly regarded by Pope Innocent IV. One day he went to the pope's rooms, where assistants were tallying large sums of money. The pope said to Aquinas, "You see, the church is no longer in an age when she must say like Peter, 'Silver and gold have I none.'"

"It is true, Holy Father," replied Aquinas. "Nor can she now say to the lame man, 'Rise and walk.'"

- Adapted from Walter Baxendale's *Dictionary of Anecdote, Incident, Illustrative Fact*. New York: Thomas Whittaker, 1889.

Frightening invention. ALBERT THE GREAT constructed a curious mechanism, which emitted distinct vocal sounds. Thomas Aquinas was so terrified at it, that he whacked it with his staff, smashing it. Albert was mortified, for the ingenious contraption had taken him 30 years to perfect!

- From Isaac D'Israeli's *Curiosities of Literature*. London: Frederick and Warne, 1881.

Argyll, Marquis of (1607-1661). Reply at Sentencing.

Archibald Campbell, the 8th Marquis of Argyll, a Covenanter, was a staunch defender of Scottish religious and political liberties. His role in the Civil War and after defies easy analysis.

AFTER THE RESTORATION, the Marquis of Argyll presented himself at Whitehall, seeking reconciliation with Charles II, who instead placed him on trial. The trial seemed likely to go Argyll's way until a turncoat friend produced some letters which showed Argyll had collaborated with the Commonwealth to put down a Royalist uprising. These sealed his doom. His words upon hearing the sentence left no doubt of his faith: "You have the indemnity of an earthly king among your hands, and have denied me a share in that; but you cannot hinder me from the indemnity of the King of Kings. Shortly you must stand before His tribunal; and I pray He may not measure out such measure to you as you have done to me, when you are called to account for your actions, including this. I had the honor to set the crown upon the King's head, and now he hastens me to a crown greater than his own."

- Adapted from James Taylor's *The Scottish Covenanters*. London: Cassell, [1880].

Arnauld, Antoine (1612-1694). When Can We Rest?

A leader of the Jansenists (a Catholic reform movement), Arnauld was also a great controversialist, whose run-ins with the Jesuits eventually got him exiled from France.

ARNAULD'S REMARKABLE REPLY to his friend Nicolle, when they were hunted from place to place, should never be forgotten. He wished Nicolle to assist him in a new work, but the latter observed, "We are now old, is it not time to rest?"

"Rest!" exclaimed Arnauld, "have we not all Eternity to rest in?"

- From Isaac D'Israeli's *Curiosities of Literature*. London: Frederick and Warne, 1881.

Asbury, Francis (1745-1816). Excerpts from Journal.

Coming from England, Asbury built up the Methodists from one of the smallest sects in America to one of the largest, becoming their first bishop. Always near poverty, he achieved his success through ceaseless vigilance and hard work.

September 12, 1771. Thoughts on sailing for America. I WILL SET DOWN a few things that lie on my mind. Whither am I going? To the New World. What to do? To gain honor? No, if I know my own heart. To get money? No; I am going to live to God, and to bring others so to do. ...If God does not acknowledge me in America, I will soon return to England. I know my views are upright now; may they never be otherwise!

September 8, 1776. The importance of prayer. MY PRESENT practice is to set apart about three hours out of every twenty-four for private prayer; but Satan labors much to interrupt me.

September 14, 1783. Sleeping on a plank while sick. I INJURED MYSELF by speaking too long and too loud. I rode seven miles, got wet, had poor lodgings with plenty of mosquitoes; next day, poorly as I was, I had to ride seventeen miles, and spoke while I had a high fever on me. I laid me down on a plank; hard lodging this for a sick man.

December 25, 1787. Filled with the Spirit on Christmas Eve. LAST NIGHT while sleeping I dreamed I was praying for sanctification, and God very sensibly filled me with love, and I waked shouting, "Glory, glory to God!" My soul was all in a flame. I had never felt so much of God in my life; and so I continued. This is Christmas Day—a great day to me. I rode to the widow Wollord's, and preached on, "For this purpose the Son of God was manifested, that he might destroy the works of the devil." During the last five days we have ridden one hundred and forty miles.

October 14, 1803. A rough road and lack of amenities. WHAT A ROAD have we passed! Certainly the worst on the whole continent, even in the best weather. Yet, bad as it was, there were four or five hundred crossing the rude hills while we were. I was powerfully struck with the consideration that there were at least as many thousand immigrants annually from East to West. We must take care to send preachers after these people. We have made one thousand and eighty miles from Philadelphia; and now, what a detail of sufferings I might give, fatiguing to me to write, and perhaps to my friends to read. A man who is well mounted will scorn to complain of the roads when he sees men, women and children, almost naked, paddling barefoot and barelegged along, or laboring up the rocky hills, while those who are best off have only a horse for two or three children to ride at once. If these adventurers have little or nothing to eat, it is no extraordinary circumstance, and not uncommon, to encamp in the wet woods after night—in the mountains it does not rain, but pours. I too have my sufferings, perhaps peculiar to myself—no room to retire to; that in which you sit is common to all, crowded with women and children, the fire occupied by cooking, much and long-loved solitude not to be found, unless you choose to run out into the rain, in the woods. Six months of the year I have had, for thirty-two years, occasionally, to submit to what will never be agreeable to me; but the people, it must be confessed, are among the kindest souls in the world. But kindness will not make a crowded log cabin, twelve feet by ten, agreeable; without are cold and rain, and within six adults and as many children, one of which is all motion; the dogs, too, must sometimes be admitted. On Saturday, I found that among my other trials I had taken an uncomfortable skin disease; and, considering the filthy houses and filthy beds I have met with, in coming from Kentucky Conference, it is perhaps strange that I have not caught it twenty times. I do not see that there is any security against it, but by sleeping in a brimstone shirt...

September 20, 1806. Giving the shirt off his back. THE BRETHREN WERE IN WANT, and could not provide clothes for themselves, so I parted with my watch, my coat, and my shirt.

- Francis Asbury. *The Heart of Asbury's Journal; being the substance of the printed journals of the Reverend Francis Asbury* ... Edited by Ezra Squier Tipple, D.D. New York, Eaton & Mains; Cincinnati, Jennings & Graham, 1904.

Askew, Anne (1521-1546). No Denial.

Anne Askew was martyred for her Protestant beliefs during the English Reformation, after tortures that left her so broken she had to be carried to the stake in a chair.

OFFERED ONE LAST CHANCE to escape the flames by renouncing her beliefs, Anne replied, "I came not here to deny my Lord and Master."

- Adapted from Walter Baxendale's *Dictionary of Anecdote, Incident, Illustrative Fact.* New York: Thomas Whittaker, 1889; also *Foxe's Book of Martyrs, Select Works of John Bale,* and Bainton's *Women of the Reformation.*

Athanasius (ca. 293-373). Christ's Champion Accused of Magic.

At the council of Nicea, Athanasius spoke boldly against the Arian heresy which would have diminished Christ to the stature of a merely created being. In so doing, he made enemies who never forgot or forgave. When he became bishop of Alexandria, they attacked him with one serious accusation after another, including charges of murder. Many times his life was threatened. Five times he was forced into exile. Nothing he could do or say, no level of proof, ever was sufficient to entirely vindicate himself from false charges.

ANY DREAMS OF QUIET which Athanasius may have entertained were rudely broken. These were days of superstition, and the people's credulity was played upon in the next charge brought against the Alexandrian bishop. Arsenius, a Meletian bishop, went into hiding, and rumors said that Athanasius had caused him to be murdered.  The claim went forth that one of the dead man's hands had been secured by Athanasius for magical purposes. His enemies exhibited a human hand in a wooden box as the very hand of the murdered Arsenius.

The friends of Athanasius were on the lookout for treachery, and sought Arsenius' hiding place. Having ascertained his whereabouts in a certain monastery on the eastern side of the Nile, they attempted to secure his person, but informants warned him in time to evade those seeking him. Later, however, Arsenius was discovered in Tyre. At first he denied his identity, but later was forced to confess that he was no other than himself.

Constantine had summoned Athanasius to Antioch for trial, upon hearing the charge of murdering Arsenius, but when he learned that Arsenius was alive, he dismissed the case in disgust. Such a succession of attempt and failure ought to have been enough to discourage the enemies of the bishop of Alexandria. But they had a steadiness of purpose worthy of a better cause. Failure only seemed to spur them on to resume the attack. Their hatred was unrelenting, and they never wavered in their purpose to ruin Athanasius.

The emperor was persuaded that there was enough root in the charges to submit the case to a council. This was to have met at Caesarea. Athanasius distrusted the fairness of those who were to try his case, and refused to attend. This was a bold stand and was sure to be used against him.

The emperor celebrated the thirtieth year of his reign in 335 by the dedication of a great church on Mt. Calvary. Before the bishops went to Jerusalem they held a council at Tyre, and commanded Athanasius to attend. This time there was no refusing, and he appeared at Tyre attended by fifty of his subordinates. His enemies had a majority and from the first he and his bishops received rude treatment. Macarius, a subordinate of Athanasius who was falsely accused of overturning an altar table while a priest was giving the sacrament, was dragged before the council in chains and Athanasius forced to appear as defendant, answering to worn out charges, with new charges thrown in to insure his final discomfiture.

When the story of the murder of Arsenius was once more hurled at him, Athanasius inquired if any present knew Arsenius. Many replied that they did. Athanasius led out a man with face closely covered. When he told him to raise his head, those present beheld Arsenius before them. This was a brilliant stroke, and when first one hand and then the other was drawn from the man's cloak, Athanasius ironically remarked that he did not suppose God had given more than two hands to any man. One of those principally concerned in the Arsenius charge was so taken aback by all this that he fled from the room. Others, however, appealed to superstition, and cried out that it was an illusion of magic. This so influenced the crowd that Athanasius barely escaped with his life.

- Adapted from Lynn Harold Hough's *Athanasius: the Hero*. Cincinnati, Ohio: Jennings and Graham, 1906.

Augustine of Hippo (354-430). Escapes an Ambush.

Little need be said of Augustine, the best-known and most influential theologian between the days of the early church and the Renaissance. After his conversion, he served as bishop of Hippo.

FIFTH CENTURY NORTH AFRICA was torn by a bitter religious strife. While Augustine and his fellow-bishops preached peace, Donatist bishops urged their followers to a holy war. Augustine received threats on his life. During one of his visitations to the churches under his care, he narrowly escaped assassination. Men lay in ambush along the route he was to take. His guide took a wrong turn, and Augustine owed his life to this mistake.

The treatment he could have expected is shown in what the Donatists did to others. For instance, the Donatist bishop Crispinus and his mob cornered Augustine's pupil Possidius, Bishop of Guelma, in a house. Possidus defended himself desperately, but the Donatists set fire to the house to burn him out. When there was nothing else left but to burn alive, he did come out. The Donatists seized him, and would have beaten his brains out, if Crispinus had not interfered, fearing a prosecution for murder. Nonetheless, the assailants sacked the property and slaughtered all the horses and mules in the stables.

At Bagai, thugs stabbed Bishop Maximianus in his basilica. A furious mob smashed the altar and began to strike their victim with the fragments, leaving him for dead on the flagstones. The Catholics then lifted up his body, but the Donatists plucked him out of their hands and flung him from the top of a tower. Fortunately, he fell on a dunghill which broke his fall. The unhappy man was still breathing, and by a miracle he recovered.

- Adapted from Louis Bertrand's *Saint Augustin*. Public domain.

Aylward, Gladys (1902-1970). What's In a Name?

Gladys Aylward was a London maid who longed to go as a missionary to China, but was told by a mission society she was too stupid. So she saved her money and went on her own, and became eminently successful, experiencing deep hardships but loving people into the kingdom of Christ.

AT A TIME when Gladys felt especially lonely and was praying for companionship, she saw a sick, sore-covered child lying in the sun where it must soon die. She scolded the woman who let it lie in neglect. "So what if it dies," replied the woman. "I can buy another tomorrow or the day after." She offered the baby to Gladys for two shillings (about 28¢).

Gladys was horrified, but a Mandarin with her said nothing could be done. Thousands perished daily in China of such neglect.

When they returned from their business, the child was still there. The woman came up to Gladys. "You can have her for a shilling," she said.

Gladys could not bear the sight of the neglected baby. She felt in her pocket and found she had five small Chinese coins. "This is all I have," she said, holding them out to the woman.

The woman snatched the coins and Gladys had her first orphan. She named the little girl "Ninepence" because that was the value of the coins that purchased her.

- Retold from the account in Gladys Aylward's *The Small Woman of the Inn of the Sixth Happiness*. Chicago: Moody Press, 1970.

Bach, Johann Sebastian (1685-1750). Night Music.

Johann Sebastian Bach is considered one of the greatest composers who ever lived. A Lutheran, he used considerable Pietist material in his chorales and other vocal compositions.

LEFT AN ORPHAN when not quite ten years old, Bach was dependent on his oldest brother, Johann Christoph, who gave him his first lessons on the clavier. His inclination and talent for music were already pronounced; his brother had no sooner gave him one piece to learn that the boy was demanding another more difficult. The most renowned clavier composers of the day were Froberger, Fischer, Kerl, Pachelbel, Buxtehude, Bruhns, and Böhm. Johann Christoph possessed a book with pieces by these masters, and Bach begged earnestly for it, but without success. For some reason his brother denied it to him and locked it up.

Refusal increasing his determination, Bach planned to get the book in spite of his brother. It was kept on a shelf with a latticed front. Bach's hands were small. Inserting them, he got hold of the book, rolled it up and drew it out. As he was not allowed a candle, he could only copy it on moonlit nights, and it was six months before he finished his heavy task. As soon as it was completed, he looked forward to using in secret a treasure won by so much labor. But his brother found the copy and took it from him without mercy, nor did Bach recover it until his brother's death soon after.

- Adapted from Johann Nikolaus Forkel's *Johann Sebastian Bach, His Life, Art and Work;* translated with notes and appendices by Charles Sanford Terry. New York: Harcourt, Brace and Howe, 1920.

Basil (ca. 329-379). Dangerous Answers.

Basil, Bishop of Caesarea, ranks as one of the greatest fourth century church fathers, the defender of orthodoxy, and the first to form monks into a force for the active transformation and betterment of society.

Reply to Valens. EMPEROR VALENS WAS AN ARIAN, denying the divinity of Christ, whereas Basil defended the Trinity. When Valens came to Caesarea, the local prefect sent for Basil and commanded him to embrace the religious sentiments of the emperor, threatening him with death in case of non-compliance. "Would that I might be released from the bonds of the body for the truth's sake," replied Basil.

The prefect gave him the rest of the day and the approaching night for deliberation, and advised him not to rush imprudently into obvious danger, but told him to come on the following day and declare his opinion. "I do not require time to deliberate," replied Basil. "My determination will be the same tomorrow as it is today; for since I am a creature I can never be induced to worship that which is similar to myself and worship it as God; neither will I conform to your religion, nor to that of the emperor. Although your distinction may be great, and you have the honor of ruling no inconsiderable portion of the empire, yet I ought not on these accounts seek to please men, and, at the same time, belittle that Divine faith which neither loss of goods, nor exile, nor condemnation to death would ever impel me to betray. Inflictions of this nature have never excited in my mind one pang of sorrow. I possess nothing but a cloak and a few books. I dwell on the earth as a traveler." As for torture, he pointed out that his body, by its weakness, would soon have victory through death.

The death of the emperor's son at about this time was widely regarded as a judgment on Valens for threatening Basil and refusing to convert to the true faith, and the emperor and his agent, subdued by the event, did not carry out their threats.

* Adapted from accounts in Socrates and Rufinus, the church historians.

Reply to Julian. JULIAN ASCENDED THE THRONE and desired to surround himself with the associates of his early days. Among the first whom he invited was his fellow-student at Athens, Basil. Basil considered accepting his old friend's invitation; but hesitated, and Julian's return to paganism gave Basil good reason to reject the opportunity. The next year Julian displayed his irritation. Receiving intelligence that the people of Caesarea, so far from apostatizing with him and building new pagan temples, had pulled down the only one still standing, he erased Caesarea from the catalogue of cities, made it take its old name of Mazaca, imposed heavy payments, compelled the clergy to serve in the police force, and put to death two young men of high rank who had taken part in the demolition of the temple. Approaching Caesarea, he dispatched a letter to Basil demanding a thousand pounds of gold for the expenses of his Persian expedition, threatening if he did not receive the money to raze the city to the ground. Basil, in his reply, reproached the emperor for apostasy against God and the church, and for his folly in demanding so vast a sum from him, the poorest of the poor. The death of Julian delivered Basil from this imminent peril.

* Adapted from Henry Wace's *A Dictionary of Christian Biography and Literature to the End of the Sixth Century A.D., with an Account of the Principal Sects and Heresies*. Public domain.

Baxter, Richard (1615-1691). Lesson from a Scare.

Richard Baxter was an English Puritan church leader and the author of many books, including The Saints' Everlasting Rest.

RICHARD BAXTER WAS PREACHING one Sunday in St. Dunstan's Church, which was very old, when something fell in the steeple.

Terrified, the people ran out of church in wild disorder. In the midst of the confusion, Baxter, without any visible emotion, sat down in the pulpit. When the fright was over, and the congregation somewhat calmed, he resumed his sermon, saying, "We are in the service of God, to prepare ourselves, that we may be fearless at the great noise of the dissolving world, when the heavens shall pass away, and the elements melt with fervent heat, the earth also, and the works therein shall be burnt up."

• Adapted from Sholto and Reuben Percy. *The Percy Anecdotes.* Harper & Brothers, 1847.

Bede (ca. 672- 735). His Godly Death.

Bede was a monk at Wearmouth and Jarrow, and the Father of English History.

ON TUESDAY BEFORE THE ASCENSION he began to be much worse in his breathing, and a small swelling appeared in his feet; but he passed all that day pleasantly, and dictated in school, saying now and then, "Go on quickly; I don't know how long I shall hold out, or whether my Maker will soon take me away." To us he seemed very well to know the time of his departure. He spent the night awake in thanksgivings.

On Wednesday morning he ordered us to write speedily what he had begun [a translation of the Gospel of John]. After this, we made the procession according to the custom of that day, walking with the relics of the saints till the third hour, then one of us said to him: "Most dear master, there is still one chapter wanting. Do you think it troublesome to be asked more questions?"

He answered: "It is no trouble. Take your pen and write quickly." The writer did so. But at the ninth hour (three in the afternoon) Bede said to me: "Run quickly; and bring all the priests of the monastery to me."

When they came, he distributed to them some pepper-corns, little cloths or handkerchiefs, and incense which he had in a little box, entreating every one that they would carefully celebrate masses and say prayers for him; which they readily promised to do. They all wept at his telling them they should no more see his face in this world; but rejoiced to hear him say: "It is now time for me to return to him who made me, and gave me a being when I was nothing. I have lived a long time; my merciful Judge most graciously foresaw and ordered the course of my life for me. The time of my dissolution draws near. I desire to be dissolved, and to be with Christ. Yes; my soul desires to see Christ my king in his beauty."

Many other things he spoke to our edification, and spent the rest of the day in joy till the evening. The above-mentioned young scholar, whose name was Wilberth, said to him: "Dear master, there is still one sentence that is not written."

He answered, "Write quickly."

The young man said: "It is now done."

He replied: "You have well said; it is at an end: all is finished. Hold my head, that I may have the pleasure of sitting and looking towards my little oratory where I used to pray; that while I am sitting I may call upon my heavenly Father, and on the pavement of this little place sing, 'Glory be to the Father, and to the Son, and to the Holy Ghost.'" Thus he prayed on the floor, and when he had named the Holy Ghost, he breathed out his soul.

- Adapted from Alban Butler's *The Lives or the Fathers, Martyrs and Other Principal Saints.* D. & J. Sadlier, & Company, 1864.

Bernard of Clairvaux (1090-1153). Against Pluralities.

The French abbot Bernard of Clairvaux, was a motivator of men and influential in the development of the Cistercians and the promotion of the crusades.

ST. BERNARD, being consulted by one of his followers whether he might accept two benefices, replied, "And how will you be able to serve them both?"

"I intend," answered the priest, "to officiate in one of them by a deputy."

"Will your deputy suffer eternal punishment for you too?" asked the saint. "Believe me, you may serve your cure by proxy, but you must suffer the penalty in person."

- Recounted by Oliver Maillard.

Berridge, John (1716-1793). Forgetfulness.

John Berridge, the vicar of Everton, went by the nickname "Old Devil" among enemies, who hated his clear Gospel preaching.

ON ONE OCCASION, while mounting the stairs of the pulpit at Tottenham Court Road, his memory seemed to fail him, and he commenced his sermon by saying, "I set out to this place tonight with a sack well filled with well-baked wheaten bread, which I hoped to set before you, but the bottom came out of the sack as I walked upstairs, and I have nothing left for you but five barley loaves and a few small fishes. You will have those loaves hot from the oven; may they be food convenient for your souls."

- From Charles Spurgeon's *Eccentric Preachers*. London: Passmore and Alabaster, 1879.

Bowles, Charles (1751-1843). Braving the Bullies.

As an African-American, Charles Bowles, a Freewill Baptist evangelist in New England, experienced racial prejudice.

IN HUNTINGTON, VERMONT, Charles Bowles baptized converts in a lake near where he preached. Some young men plotted to mount him on a wooden horse and fling him into that lake.

Fortifying themselves with whiskey and painting their faces (while he fortified himself in prayer), they came to the meeting. At the end of the service, he said, "I am informed that there are certain persons in this house, who have agreed to put me on a wooden horse, carry me to the pond and throw me in; and now dear creatures, I shall make no resistance at all—I am all ready; but before starting I have one request to make. I wish you to put one of your most resolute men forward, because I have another subject from God to preach on the way; and we will have music as we go along, glory be to God, yes we will have music; glory be to God."

His opponents came under such conviction some literally dropped to the floor. Several were converted. Instead of dunking him in the lake, they themselves were dunked there—in baptism.

- Adapted from John W. Lewis' *The Life, Labors, and Travels of Elder Charles Bowles of the Free Will Baptist Denomination*. Watertown: Ingalls & Stowell's Steam Press, 1852.

Bradford, William (1589-1657). A Christmas Day Tiff.

The weight of managing the Pilgrim colony at Plymouth fell suddenly upon William Bradford when its elected leader John Carver died unexpectedly just a few weeks after the Mayflower *sailed back to England. Bradford proved up to the challenge. His* Journal *is an important source of information from the early settlement. It shows a man generally respectful of others' beliefs. Bradford's Pilgrims did not believe in celebrating Christmas.*

ON CHRISTMAS, Bradford called the colonists out to work as usual, but most of the newcomers excused themselves and said it went against their consciences to work on that day. So he told them that if they made it matter of conscience, he would spare them from work until they were better informed. Bradford led away the rest and left the newcomers behind; but when the workers returned home at noon, they found the newcomers in the street playing; some pitching the bar and some bowling, and similar sports. So he took away their implements, and told them that it was against *his* conscience that they should play while others worked. If they made keeping Christmas Day a matter of devotion, he said, let them stay in their houses, but there would be no gaming or reveling in the streets. After that, nothing was attempted in that way, at least openly.

• Adapted from William Bradford's *Journal*.

Brand, Evelyn Harris (1879-1974). The Horse Knows the Way.

Evelyn "Granny" Brand was a missionary to India where her husband Jesse died of blackwater fever. She continued his work.

EVIE HAD ALWAYS BEEN TIMID ABOUT RIDING Jesse's horse. After he died, she determined to carry on his work, and the horse seemed a key to success, because it could give her greater speed.

Jesse had promised to revisit a certain distant village and Evie set out to keep his promise for him. In places, the path was treacherous, hugging a sheer precipice and requiring a ride over outcropping rocks. She had trembled to pass here even when Jesse was with her. Shortly before he died, he had told her he'd found a much safer route to the village. "Now he will never be able to show me," she thought.

As she struggled with her grief, she slackened the reins. Jesse's horse turned from the usual stony path into the jungle, carried Evie through the forest, over a stream, and into the village by the new path Jesse had found—a path the animal had only traveled once.

- Retold from Dorothy Clarke Wilson's *Granny Brand; Her Story*. New York: Christian Herald Books, 1976.

Brand, Paul (1914-2003). Night of Leprosy.

Paul Brand was a missionary-doctor in India, who pioneered the treatment of leprosy, and proved that the insensitivity of leprous tissues made them susceptible to injury and rot, rather than leprosy itself. He won prestigious awards, and, in conjunction with Philip Yancey, wrote several books highlighting the religious implication of modern medicine.

IN 1952, PAUL BRAND ARRIVED EXHAUSTED to visit an aunt in London after researching and lecturing in the United States, where he had contracted a severe flu-like illness. Still weakened from it, he made the transatlantic crossing and the train ride to London. In his bedroom he pulled off his shoes and socks and discovered to his horror that the had no sensation in one heel. It was the darkest moment in his life to that point. Apparently he had contracted leprosy, something he had considered unlikely, but had always feared. He drove a pin into the affected area, but felt no sensation.

All night he lay awake, trying to decide what he must do with his life, and his family. When the morning turned gray, he rose. Determined to the learn the extent of the damage, he drove in another pin—and yelped with pain. He fell to his knees and praised God; he did not have leprosy after all. Exhausted by his journey, he had sat unmoving for too long and numbed a nerve.

The experience made him more conscious of the mental suffering of those who experience leprosy and eventually led him to write *Pain, the Gift Nobody Wants*.

- Derived from Paul Brand's *Pain, the Gift Nobody Wants*. Zondervan, 1993; and Dorothy Clarke Wilson's *Ten Fingers for God*. New York: McGraw-Hill, 1965.

Bray, Billy (1794-1868). Suited to Fit.

Billy Bray was a rough and drunken Cornish tin-miner at his conversion. He became a bold and humorous soul-winner.

A KIND-HEARTED member of the Society of Friends (Quakers) once approached Billy Bray and said in his quaint Quaker way, "I have often observed thy unselfish life, and feel much interested in thee, and I believe the Lord would have me help thee; so if thou wilt call at my house I have a suit of clothes, to which thou art very welcome if they will fit thee."

"Thank'ee," replied Billy; "I will call; thee need have no doubt that the clothes will fit me. If the Lord told thee that they were for me, they're sure to fit, for He knows my size exactly."

- Adapted from Walter Baxendale's *Dictionary of Anecdote, Incident, Illustrative Fact*. New York: Thomas Whittaker, 1889.

Brown, Samuel Robbins (1810-1880). Facing Down School Bullies.

Rev. S. R. Brown was renowned as an educator, especially in the Orient, where he prepared the hearts and minds of men influential in the Protestant church at Yokohama, helped translate the New Testament into Japanese, and opened Japan's first Protestant theological seminary. William Griffis recounts the pluck with which Brown faced an assignment as a young teacher in Wales, Massachusetts.

THE VILLAGE, seven miles from Monson, was hardly a prepossessing place at that day. The church building, then in its paintless, dilapidated appearance, was a fitting representation of the religious condition of the community...

On his arrival he was told that the school was a difficult one to manage, and that the winter previous the master had been pitched out into the snow by some of the big boys. "But I never knew what it was to be afraid of my pupils. Not that I was strong and muscular, but I felt I could manage them." On the first morning he forestalled any attempt at insult by making a pleasant speech. Looking into the bright and intelligent faces around him, he told the lads that he had probably been misinformed, and that they had been slandered. However, if anyone wished to try the same trick upon him, then and there was the time to settle the question. No champion stepped forward and Brown had no trouble.

- William Elliot Griffis. *A Maker of the New Orient*. New York: Fleming H. Revell, 1902.

Bunyan, John (1628-1688). The Vanishing Flute.

John Bunyan, celebrated author of Pilgrim's Progress, was often imprisoned for preaching without license from the English established church.

TO PASS AWAY the gloomy hours in prison, Bunyan took a rail out of the stool belonging to his cell, and, with his knife, fashioned it into a flute.

The keepers, hearing music, followed the sound to Bunyan's cell; but, while they were unlocking the door, the ingenious prisoner replaced the rail in the stool, so that the searchers were unable to solve the mystery; nor, during the remainder of Bunyan's residence in the jail, did they ever discover how the music had been produced.

Robert Chambers. *The Book of Days; a miscellany of popular antiquities in connection with the calendar, including anecdote, biography, & history, curiosities of literature and oddities of human life and character.* Edinburgh, W. & R. Chambers; Philadelphia, J.B. Lippincott & Co., 1863-64.

Byles, Dr. Mather (1707-1788). Puns and Farce.

Mather Byles, an American clergyman and poet, was ousted by his church because of his loyalty to Britain during the Revolutionary War. He met all such circumstances with good humor.

AT THE TIME of the American Revolution, there was a preacher, a delightful old wit and Tory, named Dr. Mather Byles. His sympathies were frankly loyal, and he kept on praying for the King and "consorting" with British officers until his congregation very logically concluded that he was no longer suited to pray publicly for them; and in 1776, dissolved his connection with them. But all through the years of his pastorate, good stories about him were always flying over the Province, to be repeated at every table. His puns are as intrinsic a part of New England history as those of Lamb and Sydney Smith in the literature of England. Tudor's stories about him are perennially good. Doubtless his people would have made him, like his colleagues, commit himself in the pulpit on the subject of politics, that they might have him on the hip; but he was not to be beguiled.

"I have," said he, "thrown up four breastworks, behind which I have entrenched myself, none of which can be forced. In the first place, I do not understand politics; in the second place, you all do, every man and mother's son of you; in the third place, you have politics all the week (pray, let one day in seven be devoted to religion); in the fourth place, I am engaged in a work of infinitely greater importance; give me any subject to preach on of more consequence than the truths I bring you, and I will preach on it the next Sabbath."

He was of all men "good at the uptake," and perpetually ready. Having been denounced, he was tried and confined for a time in his own house. One day he persuaded the sentinel to do an errand for him, while he kept guard; and the townspeople were amused beyond measure at seeing the doctor "very gravely marching before his door, the musket on his shoulder, keeping guard over himself." It was he who, assigned one sentinel after another, and finally left to his own devices, remarked that he had been "guarded, re-guarded, and disreguarded." It was he who, when two of the selectmen stuck fast in a slough, and alighted to pull out their chaise, said to them respectfully, "Gentlemen, I have often complained to you of this nuisance without any attention being paid to it, and I am very glad to see you stirring in the matter now."

It was he who, on the Dark Day of 1780, returned word to a timorous matron who had sent her son to him for spiritual or scientific explanation, "My dear, you will give my compliments to your mamma, and tell her that I am as much in the dark as she is."

• Alice Brown. *Mercy Warren*. New York: Charles Scribner's Sons, 1896.

Calvin, John (1509-1564). Generosity and Self-Respect in Poverty; Sunday Amusements.

When the eminent theologian and reformer John Calvin was driven from Geneva after his first sojourn there, he taught theology at Strasbourg for a pittance. This first anecdote reveals his character regarding that transaction. The second shows that he was not so rigid as to forbid play, even on the Lord's Day.

Strasbourg poverty. THE LEADERS OF THE CHURCH gave him their confidence and open arms, and he received the appointment by the Council of professor of theology, with a small salary accompanying. That it was insufficient we are not in doubt, and only the proffered kindness of an intimate friend, du Tillet, revealed to the deeply-wounded and chagrined scholar that he need not depend upon official support, if only he would become content to withhold himself from public activity. This Calvin could not do, and he declined the aid of his old friend, who, by the way, was now turning his face back to Romanism. Calvin's financial distress was often very real. To make ends meet he swelled the fifty-two florins of annual salary he got from the authorities, by boarding young French students. To his beloved Farel he wrote: "I am so needy, that I have not a cent in my pocket. You will be unwilling to credit how expensive it is to keep house."

Farel managed to send him some money for lifting the temporary burden. But the proud-spirited Calvin made it a condition that he should accept no more than he could hope to repay within a reasonable time. He worked on, not infrequently without the plainest necessities of life, but noted for a remarkable generosity which gave to others everything above his bare living.

- Richard Taylor Stevenson. *John Calvin: the Statesman*. Cincinnati, Ohio; Jennings and Graham, 1907.

Amusements. HIS PLEASURES WERE FEW and simple. John Knox found him playing bowls on a Sunday afternoon. "He himself made no scruple in engaging in play with the seigneurs of Geneva; but that was the innocent game of the clef (key), which consists on being able to push the keys the nearest possible to the edge of the table."

- Quoted from Bonnet's Letters in Richard Taylor Stevenson's *John Calvin: the Statesman*. Cincinnati, Ohio; Jennings and Graham, 1907.

Canute the Great (ca. 995-1035). King of Kings?

Canute (Knute or Cnut) was a Danish Christian who ruled England and most of Scandinavia and who founded many churches. This anecdote may be apocryphal; it did not appear in the earliest sources.

KING CANUTE, walking on the sands, was extolled by some of his flattering followers, who told him that he was a King of Kings, the mightiest that reigned far and near; that both land and sea were at his command.

This talk did not sit well with the Christian king, and so he determined to repel their flattery with a demonstration. He took off his cloak, and wrapping it a couple times to form a cushion, sat down on it beside the sea which was flowing in.

He then commanded, "Sea, don't touch my feet." No sooner had he spoken the words than a wave dashed upon him.

Getting up and going back, he said, "You see now, my lords, how appropriate it is for you to call me a king—I who cannot even hold back one wave by my orders. The fact is, no mortal man is worthy of such a lofty title. Only one King rules everything. Let us honor him, call him King of Kings and Lord of all Nations, Ruler of the Heavens, Sea and Land."

- Adapted from William Camden's *Remaines concerning Britain: their languages, names, surnames, allusions, anagrammes, armories, monies, empreses, apparell, artillarie, wise speeches, proverbs, poesies, epitaphs.* London: Simon Waterson and Robert Clavell, 1657. Sixth edition.

Carey, William (1761-1834). Acquires World Vision.

William Carey was an impoverished cobbler, Baptist preacher and inept teacher in the Kettering district of England when he woke to the need to reach the world for Christ. His family half starved while he studied, preached and wrote pamphlets about the subject nearest his heart: the salvation of souls at home and abroad.

GEOGRAPHY WAS HIS FAVORITE SUBJECT for teaching, and it was while he taught class from a leather globe of his own making that it flashed painfully across his mind how large a portion of the world's inhabitants were in the darkness of heathendom. The idea grew upon him until it haunted him by day and by night.  In his workshop he had upon the wall a huge map, made of many pieces of paper pasted together, on which he entered all the information he could gather regarding the population, religion, government and customs of each country. His mind was appalled at the awful need, and his spirit became heavily burdened. All his early love of travel, his largely increased knowledge of the earth and of the condition of Christian work, his study of Scripture, and his devotion to Christ were now focused into a fierce energy of love for the heathen.

In him there was nothing of that indolence which contents itself with dreams rather than with deeds. At a meeting of ministers held soon after his ordination, he suggested as a subject for their discussion, "The duty of Christian people to spread the Gospel among the heathen." He had already urged this in private among his brethren, but none were prepared for such an outburst of zeal. Even his greatest friend, Fuller, startled by the magnitude of the idea, was too amazed to speak. The elder Ryland, who had baptized him a few years earlier, rose sternly to his feet with the rebuke, "Young man, sit down! When God pleases to convert the heathen, He will do it without your aid or mine!"

Nothing daunted, he returned to his home and set himself to write a pamphlet which should embody his convictions, and entitled it, "An Enquiry into the Obligation of Christians to use Means for the Conversion of the Heathen." It was as remarkable for its cultured and finished style as for the wide knowledge it showed of the statistics and geography of the world. Race after race, country after country was surveyed, the results being tabulated with a logical exactness that compels admiration. Few men in England of that day, even with the advantages of a University training, could have produced what this obscure toiler of less than thirty years of age compiled in his tiny workshop. It was the first great missionary treatise in the English language, and it has seldom if ever been surpassed.

- Edward A. Annett. *William Carey, Pioneer Missionary to India.* London: The Sunday School Union, 1890.

Carmichael, Amy (1867-1951). Risking Much for Little.

Amy Carmichael was an Irish missionary to Japan and India, renowned for her poetry and writings. Because of her physical ailments, she preferred to wear warmer western clothes in Japan. However, she soon adopted native costume. This anecdote explains why.

WE WENT TO SEE AN OLD LADY who was very ill. She had not heard the Gospel before, but was willing and eager to listen. So I spoke and Misaki San translated, and our hearts prayed most earnestly. "Lord Jesus, help her. O help her to understand and open her heart to You now."

She seemed to be just about to turn to Him in faith when suddenly she noticed my hands. It was cold weather and I had on fur gloves. "What are these," she asked, stretching out her hand and touching mine.

She was old and ill and easily distracted. I cannot remember whether or not we were able to recall her to what mattered so much more than gloves. But this I do remember, I went home, took off my English clothes, put on my Japanese kimono, and never again, I trust, risked so very much for the sake of so very little.

- Quoted by Frank Houghton in *Amy Carmichael of Dohnavur; the story of a lover and her beloved*. Fort Washington, Pennsylvania: Christian Literature Crusade, ca. 1959.

Cartwright, Peter (1785-1872). Confounds a Highwayman; Deadly Dawn.

Peter Cartwright was a Methodist circuit rider on the American frontier late in the 18th and early in the 19th centuries. The difficulty with selecting any anecdote from his colorful Autobiography is that so many good ones have to be turned down. These two anecdotes illustrate the dangers of the frontier and how physical preachers had to be.

Encounter with a "lame" traveler. IN PASSING on our journey going down the mountains, on Monday, we met several wagons and carriages moving west. Shortly after we had passed them, I saw lying in the road a very neat pocket pistol. I picked it up, and found it heavily loaded and freshly primed. Supposing it to have been dropped by some of these movers, I said to Brother Walker, "This looks providential;" for the road across these mountains was, at this time, infested by many robbers, and several daring murders and robberies had lately been committed. Brother Walker's horse was a tolerably good one, but my horse was a stout, fleet, superior animal. As we approached the foot of the mountains, and were about two miles from the public house, where we intended to lodge that night, the sun just declining behind the western mountains, we overtook a man walking with a large stick as a walking cane, and he appeared to be very lame, and was limping along at a very slow rate. He spoke to us, and said he was traveling, and a poor cripple, and begged us to let him ride a little way, as he was nearly given out, and was fearful he could not reach the tavern that night.

Brother Walker said, "O yes," and was in the attitude of dismounting and letting him ride his horse. Just then a thought struck me, that this fellow's lameness was feigned, and that it was not safe to trust him. I said to Walker, "Keep your horse; we are a long way from home, have a long journey before us; under such circumstances, trust no man," and we trotted on down the hill, and thought we had left our lame man more than a hundred yards behind. Walker was rather ahead of me. All at once my horse made a spring forward; I turned to see what was the matter, and lo! And behold, here was my lame man, within a few steps of me, coming as fleet as a deer. I grasped my pistol, which was in my overcoat pocket, cocked it, wheeled about, and rushed toward him; he faced about and in a few jumps more I should have been on him, but he plunged into the thick brush, and I could not follow him. When we got to the tavern the landlord said we had made a very fortunate escape, for these robbers in this way had decoyed and robbed several travelers lately.

Deadly dawn. JUST BEFORE WE STRUCK the prairies, the man that drove my team contrived to turn over the wagon, and was near killing my oldest daughter. The sun was just going down; and by the time we righted up the wagon and reloaded, it was getting dark, and we had a difficult hill to descend, so we concluded to camp there for the night, almost in sight of two cabins containing families.... We laid down and slept soundly.

Just as day was appearing in the east, the tree at the root of which we had kindled a small fire fell, and it fell on our third daughter, as direct on her, from her feet to her head, as it could fall; and I suppose she never breathed after. I heard the tree crack when it started to fall, and sprang, alarmed very much, and seized it before it struck the child; but it availed nothing. Although this was an awful calamity, yet God was kind to us; for if we had stretched our tent that night, we should have been obliged to lie down in another position, and in that event the tree would have fallen directly upon us, and we should all have been killed instead of one. The tree was sound outside to the thickness of the back of a carving knife, and then all the inside had a dry rot; but this we did not suspect. I sent my teamster to those families near at hand for aid; but not a soul would come near us... My teamster and myself fell to cutting the tree off the child, when I discovered that the tree had sprung up, and did not press the child; and we drew her out from under it, and carefully laid her on our feed trough, and moved on about twenty miles to an acquaintance's in Hamilton County, Illinois, where we buried her.

• Peter Cartwright. *Autobiography*. 1856.

Carver, George Washington (1864-1943). Entomological Prank.

George Washington Carver was an eminent African-American botanist, chemurgist and educator, well-known for his Christian faith.

EVERYONE ACCEPTED THAT CARVER could identify virtually any plant brought to him, even if it was new to his eyes. His entomology class, however, thought they could stump him. They brought him a bug pinned neatly to a paper in the manner of insect specimens and asked him what the strange critter was.

He studied the insect for some time. It had the head of an ant, the body of a beetle, the legs of a spider and the antennae of a moth. Finally Carver delivered his verdict. "Well, this I think, is what we would call a humbug."

• Adapted from Rackham Holt's *George Washington Carver*. Nashville: Abingdon Press, 1943.

Chalmers, James (1841-1901). Fun on the Way to Heaven.

Robert Louis Stevenson, the famed novelist, sailed with James Chalmers in the South Seas and said of him, "He is a man nobody can see and not love." Forced to rely for transportation on the notorious captain Bully Hayes after his own ship was wrecked, Chalmers asked permission to preach evening and morning. Hayes was so taken by Chalmers that he not only granted permission but required his whole wicked crew to attend. In Papua, Chalmers won many converts to Christ before ending his life as the main course of a cannibal feast.

NO ACCOUNT OF CHALMERS at Chestnut College, however, would be complete without reference to his fellow students, and indeed to some of the frolics in which from time to time they were associated. Among the men of his time, Chalmers was a universal favorite. His  manliness, his sincerity, his simplicity endeared him to us all. There was in him that touch of nature that made him "family." To use John Henry Newman's favorite motto, it was a relationship of "heart to heart." Men might think little of his intellectual equipment, but every noble soul recognized the greatness of his heart.

Chalmers was usually the ringleader in the practical jokes of his time. Some will perhaps think that in a college of theology such things should be unknown. May I tell them for their comfort that most of the men who have been conspicuous for devoted work in after years, had, at some time or other, some part in practical joking? A too demure childhood is not a good augury for the after life. And a too serious behavior at college is not always the precursor of the most devoted work in the service of Jesus Christ. A little harmless effervescence shows that there is abundance of life; and the life of Chalmers was so abounding that it demanded expression. Long-sustained thought or study was impossible to him, and so in the interval between an early tea and supper, occupied by most men in preparation for class, he often grew restless and would wander the corridors bent on some harmless mischief, to the disturbance of the more studiously inclined.

I remember how one evening when an extra bad fit of restlessness was on him his much disturbed neighbors resolved on condign punishment. He was closely fastened in his room—the key-hole filled with cayenne pepper, to which a match was applied, so that for him to breathe was impossible, and he had to throw wide his window and put out his head to get air; but as soon as his head was out a volley of water was fired upon it from a sentinel stationed on the roof above. Such punishment, however, neither aroused his revenge nor cured his restlessness...

Who, for instance, that was at Chestnut at the time can forget the awful apparition of the great brown bear? Chalmers had made the acquaintance of Mr. Tugwell, curate at Goff's Oak. Mr. Tugwell had been for a time a missionary among the North American Indians, and had brought home with him some interesting curios. Among others, there was an enormous bear's skin, with the head and paws complete, prepared by the Indians to be worn in some of their dances. Chalmers promptly borrowed the skin, and brought it down by night to the college. He confided his secret to only one or two confederates, and at the close of a very quiet evening, when prayers were over, and the men were all in the dining hall at supper, the door was suddenly flung open and the bear appeared, standing on its hind legs, and roaring ominously. It shambled quickly into the room among the startled students, made for one of the quietest, subjected him to a terrible hug, and then pursued others. At this juncture a confederate turned out the gas and the scene of excitement in the dark may be better imagined than described. When the light was turned on, it was discovered that it Chalmers who was masquerading in this fashion. For a week after, that bear was the central subject of numerous jokes. I shall never forget the abject terror on the face of an old Irishman who used to come into the College as a vendor of fruit and other luxuries, when the bear suddenly met him at the end of the corridor, and seized him and his basket in its ample embrace.

- Richard Lovett. *James Chalmers; His autobiography and letters.* Oxford: The Religious Tract Society, 1902.

Charlemagne (died 814). The Spider Man.

Notker the Stammerer, who died in 912, compiled a number of stories relating to Charlemagne and his contemporaries. Many of these tales are credulous and superstitious, but interesting for what they show of the thought of the time, as for instance, that it was considered a sign of sinfulness to groom and bathe oneself.

THERE WAS A DEACON who followed Italian customs, resisting the course of nature, for he bathed and had himself closely shaved, polished his skin, cleaned his nails, and wore his hair cut as short as if it had been skinned by a lathe. Then he put on linen and a white robe. In spite of this unsaintly behavior, because he must not miss his turn, or perhaps desiring to make a fine show, he proceeded to read the Gospel before God and His holy angels, and in the presence of that most observant king, Charles the Great. However clean the deacon's body and clothes, his heart was unclean, as events were to prove; for while he was reading the text, a spider lowered itself from the ceiling by a thread, touched the deacon's head, and ran up again. Watchful Charles saw this happen a second and a third time, but pretended not to notice, and the clerk, because of the emperor's presence, was too polite to brush off the spider with his hand, and anyhow did not know that it was a spider attacking him, but thought that it was merely the touch of a fly. So he finished reading the Gospel, and went through the rest of the office. But when he left the cathedral he soon began to swell up, and died within an hour. But Charles, who was quite scrupulous, considered himself guilty of manslaughter and did public penance, because he had seen his danger and done nothing to prevent it.

- Retold from Notker the Stammerer's *Life of Charlemagne.* Translations consulted include the Medieval Sourcebook http://www.fordham.edu/halsall/basis/stgall-charlemagne.html and Lewis Thorpe's *Einhard and Notker the Stammerer; Two Lives of Charlemagne.* Penguin, 1971.

Chesterton, G. K. (1874-1936). Absent-mindedness.

G. K. Chesterton was a journalist, social critic, and apologist famed for his use of paradox and bursts of wit (e.g.: "The Christian ideal had not been tried and found wanting; it had been found difficult and never tried"). His books include the Father Brown detective stories,

Heretics, Orthodoxy, The Everlasting Man *and several novels with Christian themes. He converted to Catholicism.*

CHESTERTON HAD AN AMAZING ABILITY to compose entire articles in his head which, when dictated, needed only minor corrections before they could be printed. Perhaps it was because of this ability to concentrate so intensely on his writings that he was absent-minded in everyday affairs. One day his wife Frances received this cryptic telegram: "Am at Market Harborough. Where should I be?"

Frances wired back, "Home."

• For more about Chesterton, see Michael Ffinch's *G. K. Chesterton; a biography*. San Francisco: Harper and Row, 1986.

Chrysostom, John (ca. 344-407). He Tricks Basil.

John Chrysostom "Golden Mouth" was a well-educated and ardent young man who turned from law to monasticism. Eventually he was compelled to become patriarch of Constantinople and died a martyr's death for his outspoken opposition to social injustice and his denunciation of royal excesses. He  *dreaded positions of spiritual leadership, however, and did all he could to duck them as this anecdote reveals.*

AT THIS TIME occurred an incident which reveals to some extent the modesty and humility of the young man, and illustrates the laxity of the age on some questions of casuistry. Meletius was banished, and, because of certain political conditions, it was thought advisable to elect a thoroughly orthodox bishop in his place. The eyes of the church were turned toward Chrysostom and Basil [not to be confused with Basil the Great]. These splendid young men seemed eminently fitted for this exalted position, and their election was publicly discussed.

At once Chrysostom was thrown into an agony of fear. He was well aware that in a matter of this kind his personal inclination and preference would not for a moment be consulted. He would be literally and hopelessly in the hands of his friends. In those unsophisticated days the office had the habit of seeking the man, and seeking him without any noticeable reference to his wishes in the matter. More than one bewildered priest had been elected and ordained bishop willy nilly. The ecclesiastical sponsors might "lay hands suddenly on no man," in deference to apostolic injunctions, but the operation was sometimes performed very vigorously and peremptorily. St. Martin, of Tours, a pagan born, was dragged from his cell in Gaul and forcibly ordained bishop. Augustine protested against his own election with tears, but he was ordained nonetheless. The patriarch of Alexandria is even now brought to Cairo in chains and under guard, as if he would strive to escape. How this Oriental timidity and repugnance has been overcome in later years, and how the intrepidity and chivalrous devotion of the modern divines, as they calmly dare the hazardous office of bishop, might shame the fearsome patriarchs of the elder day.

On consultation, the two friends agreed to act together, either in accepting or refusing the office. Chrysostom, however, deliberately deceived Basil, concealing himself from the messengers who had been sent to bring him to the Council, and allowed them to tell Basil that he had yielded, and that they would be consecrated together. Thus Basil was entrapped and ordained and Chrysostom escaped. A cold-blooded deception was practiced. There is no question about that. Indeed, Chrysostom laughingly greets his distressed and indignant friend, and ingeniously and gleefully justifies the fraud.

• Adapted from John Heston Willey's *Chrysostom: the orator*. Cincinnati, Ohio: Jennings and Graham, 1906.

Clarke, Adam (1762-1832). The Raven; Rash Vow Almost Ruins Scholar's Future.

Anyone who has used Clarke's Commentary *has benefited from the scholarship of Adam Clarke. However, Clarke was not brilliant as a child; ridicule drove him to intense application. After his conversion, he became such a popular circuit preacher that he often had to preach out of doors, the crowds exceeding the capacity of available buildings; and at his own chapel, the press of people sometimes forced him to crawl inside through a window.*

A judgmental raven. MRS. HANNAH CLARKE, Adam's mother, was a Presbyterian of the old puritanical school. She always placed the fear of God before the eyes of her children, caused them to read and reverence the scriptures, and she tried to impress the most important parts on their minds. If they did wrong, her practice was to cite the Bible to strengthen her reproofs and deepen conviction. She knew the Bible so well there was scarcely any delinquency to which she could not easily apply a verse. She seemed to find them on first opening the Bible, and would generally say, "See what God has guided my eye to in a moment."

Her own reproofs her children could in some measure bear; but when she cited the Bible, they were terrified out of their minds, for she had filled them with awe for the truth of God's word and the majesty of its Author. One day Adam disobeyed his mother, and compounded the disobedience with defiant look or gesture. This was an insult to her; immediately she turned to the Bible and opened it to Proverbs 30:17: "The eye that mocks at his father, and despises to obey his mother, the ravens of the valley shall pick out, and the young eagles shall eat."

The poor culprit was cut to the heart, believing that the words had been sent straight from heaven. He went out into the field with a troubled spirit, and was musing on this horrible denunciation of divine displeasure, when the hoarse croak of a raven sounded to his conscience an alarm more terrible than the cry of "fire" at midnight! He looked up and spotted the ominous bird, and actually supposing it was a raven sent to pick out his eyes, clapped his hands over them in terror, and ran toward the house as fast as he could, in order to escape God's vengeance.

- George Coles. *Heroines of Methodism.* New York: Carlton & Lanahan, 1869.

Rash vow. IN THE *Life of Adam Clarke*, written by his son, an incident is related which shows how nearly this great biblical scholar had been lost to the church and the world. In 1782, while traveling the Bradford Circuit, he chanced to find a Latin sentence written on the wall of his chamber, to which he added, as being in the same vein, these lines of Virgil, changing the last word from

"Latium" to "Caelum" to suit the wanderings of the preachers rather than those of Aeneas:

> Quo fata trahunt, retrahuntque, sequamur.
> Per varios casus, per tot discrimina rerum,
> Tendimus in Caelum.

> Wherever the fates lead us, let us follow.
> Through many chances and changes of fortune,
> We press on toward Heaven.

The next preacher who saw it, by way of reproving the pride of the young scholar, wrote underneath these words: "Did you write the above to show us that you could write Latin? For shame! Do send pride to hell, from whence it came. O young man, improve your time; eternity's at hand."

On his next round, the "little boy preacher" read and accepted the reproof, and, falling on his knees, he vowed never to meddle with Greek or Latin again as long as he lived! A long time afterward, coming upon a French essay which pleased him, he translated it, and sent it to Mr. Wesley for his *Arminian Magazine,* and Wesley, who knew that ignorance and pride are twins, and that one of the best ways to drive out thoughts of self is to keep the mind full of sound knowledge, wrote to the young preacher accepting the piece, and charging him to cultivate his mind as far as circumstances would allow, and "not to forget anything he had ever learned."

Alas! through the counsel of an ignorant, ambitious, and perhaps envious itinerant, Clarke had not looked at his Greek and

Latin for nearly four years; but now he saw his error, and with the same teachable spirit, but under a better instructor, he begged the Lord to forgive his rash vow, and at once set about the task of recovering the knowledge he had nearly lost.

- W. H. Daniels. *Illustrated History of Methodism.* Methodist Book Concern, 1880.

Columba (c. 521-597). Monster Fled at Saint's Command.

We know a good deal about the Irish missionary Columba, because Adamnan recorded his life within a century of his death, using at least one earlier biography. We are fairly certain that he was responsible for a battle that killed a number of men in his homeland. He did penance by becoming a missionary to Britain where he founded a monastery on the isle of Iona, from which he and his associates converted Northern England. This extract shows the credulous manner in which Medieval writers wrote, but also raises the intriguing possibility of a Loch Ness monster.

ONCE, WHEN THE BLESSED MAN was living for some days in the province of the Picts, he was obliged to cross the river Nesa. When he reached its bank, he saw some locals burying an unfortunate man. According to them, while the man was swimming a short time before, he had been bitten by a monster that lived in the water. Too late his wretched body was taken out with a hook, by those who came to his assistance in a boat.

On hearing this, Columba was so far from being dismayed, that he directed one of his companions to swim over and bring back a fishing boat that was moored at the further bank. Lugne Mocumin, hearing the command, obeyed without the least delay, stripping off all but his tunic, and leaping into the water. The monster was lying at the bottom of the stream. Far from being satiated, it was roused for more prey, and when it felt the water disturbed above by the man swimming, rushed out, and, giving an awful roar, darted after the swimmer, with its mouth wide open. Columba, observing this, raised his holy hand, while all the rest, brethren as well as strangers, were stupefied with terror, and, invoking the name of God, formed the sign of the cross in the air, and commanded the ferocious monster, saying, "You shall go no further, nor touch the man; go back with all speed."

At the voice of the saint, the monster was terrified, and fled more quickly than if it had been pulled back with ropes, though it had got so near to Lugne, as he swam, that there was not more than the length of a spear staff between man and beast. The brethren seeing that the monster had turned back, and that their comrade Lugne returned to them in the boat safe and sound, were struck with admiration, and gave glory to God for the blessed man. Even the barbarous heathen, who were present, were forced by the greatness of this miracle, which they themselves had seen, to magnify the God of the Christians.

- Adapted from Adamnan's *Life of Saint Columba,* edited by William Reeves. Edinburgh: Edmonston and Douglas, 1874.

Cowper, William (1731-1800). John Gilpin; The Castaway.

William Cowper was a sensitive man and a brilliant and popular poet, a precursor of the Romantic movement. His poem

"John Gilpin" was one of the works which made him famous. He also authored many hymns, of which "There Is a Fountain Filled with Blood," "Oh, for a Closer Walk with God," and "God Moves in a Mysterious Way" are the best-known. Reared in strict Calvinism, he became obsessed with the notion that he was not one of the elect and therefore damned forever. His terror of this grew stronger as he approached death and exhibited itself in his symbolic poem "The Castaway."

John Gilpin. IT HAPPENED ONE AFTERNOON, in those years when Cowper's accomplished friend, Lady Austen, made a part of his little evening circle, she observed him sinking into increased dejection. It was her custom, on these occasions, to try all the resources of her sprightly powers for his immediate relief, and at this time it occurred to her to tell him the story of John Gilpin (which had been treasured in her memory from her childhood), in order to dissipate the gloom of the passing hour. Its effects on the fancy of Cowper had the air of enchantment. He informed her the next morning that convulsions of laughter, brought on by his recollection of her story, had kept him waking during the greatest part of the night! and that he had turned it into a ballad. So arose the pleasant poem of "John Gilpin."

- *The Book of Three Hundred Anecdotes Historical, Literary, and Humorous—A New Selection.* London and New York: Burns & Oates, n.d.

The Castaway. IN 1799, he wrote his last original poem, "The Castaway," founded on a passage in one of *Anson's voyages*. The poem began:

> Obscurest night involved the sky,
> The Atlantic billows roared,
> When such a destined wretch as I,
> Washing headlong from on board,
> Of friends, of hope, of all bereft,
> His floating home forever left.

Its most famous lines are:

> No voice divine the storm allay'd,
> No light propitious shone;
> When, snatch'd from all effectual aid,
> We perish'd, each alone;
> But I beneath a rougher sea,
> And whelmed in deeper gulphs than he.

He wrote the whole thing in one day. Later, when Cowper's weakness became so extreme that his death seemed near at hand, a faithful attendant ventured to speak of his approaching dissolution as the signal of his deliverance from afflictions as well of body as of mind. "After a pause of a few moments, which was less interrupted by the objections of my desponding relative than I had dared to hope, I proceeded to an observation more consolatory still, that in the world to which he was hastening, a merciful Redeemer had prepared unspeakable happiness for all His children and therefore for him [Cowper]. To the first part of this sentence he had listened with composure, but the concluding words were no sooner uttered, than he passionately expressed entreaties that I would desist from any father observations of a similar kind, which clearly proved...the darkness of delusion still veiled his spirit."

- Adapted from John S. Memes' *The Life of William Cowper*. Port Washington, New York; London: Kennikat Press, 1972, 1837; with additions from encyclopedias and anthologies.

Cranmer, Thomas (1489-1556). His Forgiving Nature; Book Ahoy! Memorial Beard.

Archbishop of Canterbury, associate of Henry VIII, reformer of England, and author of the Book of Common Prayer, Cranmer was burned at the stake under Queen Mary's rule.

His forgiving nature. THERE WAS NO TRACE of rancor in Cranmer; his friends spoke of his "incredible sweetness of manners," his enemies commended his courtesy, and his forgiving disposition became a proverb. "Do my Lord of Canterbury a shrewd (i.e., an evil) turn, writes Shakespeare, "and he is your friend forever."

"My Lord," said Heath to the Archbishop one day, "I know perfectly well how to get anything I want from you."

"How?" asked Cranmer.

"Why Sir," replied Heath, "I see that I must first try to do you some great offense, and then back off a little to get exactly what I want."

Cranmer was a little nettled at his dissection of his character. "You may be mistaken," he said to Heath. "Still, I cannot change my mind and habits, as some would have me do."

On one occasion Thomas Cromwell seized a country priest for slandering Cranmer as an ignorant ostler. The Archbishop refused to have him punished; the priest, he told Cromwell, was not the first by 500 who had called him such names, and he gently brought the man to a better understanding by showing the fellow his ignorance, and then sent him home in peace.

Book ahoy! AFTER THE PASSING of the Act of Six Articles, Henry VIII, who was genuinely interested in theological questions, asked Cranmer to provide him in writing a statement of the reasons which had led him to oppose the measure. When the manuscript was completed, Cranmer entrusted it to Morice, who happened to be crossing the Thames in a wherry, while a bear was being baited in the water. The animal broke loose, capsized Morice's boat, and the manuscript went floating down the river. It was recovered by the keeper of Princess Elizabeth's bears who tried to use it against Cranmer, but eventually it was restored to its rightful owner.

Memorial Beard. IN HIS LAST MOMENTS King Henry VIII turned to the man who had been his best friend in life; and feeling that his strength was ebbing, he sent late at night to fetch Cranmer from Croydon. When the archbishop reached Whitehall, the king was no longer able to speak; all he could do was to stretch out his hand to Cranmer and reply with an affirmative grasp when the archbishop urged him to call upon Christ's mercy and give some token that he trusted in the Lord. So died Henry VIII, and the last support of which he was conscious on earth was the hand of the man whose only support he himself had been in time of trouble. Faithless to many, to Cranmer the king was true unto death; and from that day to his own last agony, the archbishop let his beard grow in witness of his grief.

- All three anecdotes are adapted or excerpted from Albert Frederick Pollard's *Thomas Cranmer and the English Reformation*. London and New York: G. P. Putnam's Sons, 1905.

Cromwell, Oliver (1599-1658). Conversion; Dying Remembrance of Philippians Four; Loathed Images.

Oliver Cromwell was a farmer who became master of England through force of character during the English civil war between Parliament and King.

Cromwell describes his conversion. "I CAME TO the thirteenth verse, where Paul says, I can do all things through Christ who strengthens me. Then faith began to work, and my heart to find comfort and support; and I said to myself, 'He that was Paul's Christ is my Christ, too!' And so I drew water out of the wells of salvation!"

Cromwell on his death bed. BEING SICK UNTO DEATH, and in his bed chamber, Cromwell called for his Bible and desired an honorable and godly person to read unto him that passage in the fourth of Philippians which says, "I can do all things through Christ who strengthens me." When that was read, he observed, "This scripture once saved my life, when my eldest son, poor Robert, died, which went as a dagger to my heart, indeed it did!"

- Adapted from Boreham, F. W. *Life Verses,* Volume 1 (Originally titled *A Bunch of Everlastings).* Grand Rapids, Michigan: Kregel, 1994. The second story is also recounted in Walter Baxendale's *Dictionary of Anecdote, Incident, Illustrative Fact.* New York: Thomas Whittaker, 1889.

Disgust with images. WHILE VISITING one of the great churches in England, Oliver Cromwell discovered in the niches of a side chapel a number of silver statues. "What are these?" he demanded of the trembling dean who was showing him around the church.

"Please your highness," was the reply, "they are the twelve apostles."

"The twelve apostles, are they? Well, take them away at once and melt them down and coin them into money so that, like their master, they may go about doing good."

- Attributed to Reverend R. Morton; adapted from Walter Baxendale's *Dictionary of Anecdote, Incident, Illustrative Fact.* New York: Thomas Whittaker, 1889.

Cruden, Alexander (1701-1770). Creator of Concordance Saves Condemned Man.

A little mad from a time he was jilted (or perhaps jilted because he was a little mad), Alexander Cruden suffered severe compulsions. He could be annoying in his attempts to obtain his objects. For instance, he pestered girls whom he wished to marry him. He set himself to correct the morals of his time and sponged graffiti off walls. In his zeal he once became so violent he was committed to a mental hospital. It was one of several such incarcerations. His chief claim to fame was the single-handed creation of the first thorough English-language Bible concordance. He probably could not have done it and done it so quickly without a fair dose of obsessiveness. In another instance, his inability to "let go" saved a man's life.

ONE EVENING, AT A PARTY given at a cousin's house, Alexander Cruden learned that a feeble-minded sailor named Richard Potter was to be hanged for having been gulled into signing for another man's pay. He had so obviously been set up for the "crime" that London's Lord Mayor, the prosecuting lawyer, jury and others involved had recommended mercy. Their pleas were ignored by those who had final say; Richard was condemned to die.

"But it's impossible! He must not be hanged," exclaimed Cruden. "He shall be saved somehow."

Mr. Innes, the prosecutor, although he had carried out his responsibilities, had also hoped Potter might be spared. Now he said it was too late. The execution would take place in two days. Alexander prowled restlessly that night.

Early the next morning he prayed long and earnestly, then hurried to Mr. Innes' office. Innes repeated that nothing could be done. Alexander suggested a letter to the Secretary of State. Innes pleaded he did not know what to write and said the secretary would not like being disturbed. Cruden said he would draft the letter and bear it himself. Innes agreed.

Letter in hand, Cruden had himself rowed across the river to Whitehall. He had counted on the friendship of a certain under-secretary. The man was 150 miles away. Cruden was staggered. Then he remembered a clerk, Mr. Larpent, with whom he had dealt when he had presented a copy of his concordance to the king. The clerk read the letter and suggested it could be strengthened by adding some words.

Cruden rushed back to the water with the letter. On the way back to Innes' office, he stopped at his own home to fortify himself by reading a passage of scripture and falling to his knees for a quick prayer.

He then sped to the recorder's house. Innes was out. Cruden said he would wait. The recorder soon appeared but refused to sign any change. He said the matter had already been to the Privy Council and been rejected. Cruden said the recorder was mistaken. This correction made Innes angry and he refused to do more. Cruden left downcast. Yet he knew he must continue his efforts. He solicited the counsel of a friend who agreed the letter must go to Lord Halifax as it was.

Again Cruden crossed the water. He left the letter with Larpent. It was now evening and he proceeded to his place of employment where he had some editing to do. All that night he prayed for Potter.

In the morning he wrote to Larpent, pressing his request. Then it occurred to him Potter's case might be strengthened if the prison authorities would speak for the man. He hastened to Newgate and obtained a favorable testimonial from the prison's governor. Armed with this he hurried back to Larpent and asked how the letters could be gotten to Lord Halifax. Larpent advised him to carry them to Halifax's residence himself.

This seemed so bold a move that Cruden was stunned. Nonetheless, if it was the only way, he must take it. At Lord Halifax's, he met echelons of servants trained to protect their master and turn away petitioners such as himself. They buffered Lord Halifax even more than usual for at present the great man was carrying out the duties of two secretaries, another having died two days before. He was at that moment closeted with the Attorney General but Cruden finally prevailed upon a servant to at least carry his letter to Lord Halifax. Miraculously, Halifax agreed to see Cruden.

In broken tones, Cruden pleaded for the sailor. Halifax could only promise to present the matter to the king. He said when things had gone this far, there was seldom a reprieve.

Cruden had to leave the matter there. He returned home and prayed. That evening he went to Newgate to see if a reprieve had come. It had not. Sadly he returned home. He prayed some more, but, physically and emotionally exhausted, he went to bed.

At three he awoke and immediately remembered Potter. Again he prayed. That morning he went to the prison and asked to have Potter pointed out to him when he should be brought out. He continued to pray for the condemned man's soul. The wagon with the condemned men arrived. There were five, not the expected six. Hoping beyond hope, Cruden hurried to find out if Potter had been spared. To his joy, he learned that the man had been given a two-week reprieve. The prison's governor told Cruden he'd have to work quick to get the sentence changed in that short time. After what Cruden had been through in the last two days, two weeks seemed like an eternity. He proceeded home and thanked the Lord.

Cruden then got admission to see Potter. He promised him help and was as good as his word. Not only Potter benefited; Cruden was horrified by the conditions in Newgate and wrote an exposé which later resulted in reforms. Six days after Potter was to have been executed, Lord Halifax changed his sentence to transportation. Cruden's concern, backed by his obsessive personality, had won the day.

- Shortened and retold from the lengthy account in Edith Olivier's *Alexander the Corrector*. New York: Viking, 1934.

Donne, John (1573-1631). Solid Sleuthing.

John Donne was the greatest of the metaphysical poets, but poetry could not feed him. At 28 he eloped with Anne More, whose irate father immediately cut her off. Unable to obtain a satisfactory position, John and Anne lived in poverty. She died young and he blamed himself. This anecdote comes from the period in which he finally let King James persuade him to take holy orders. It was first related by Jonathan Swift.

WHEN DOCTOR DONNE, afterwards Dean of St. Paul's, London, took possession of the first living he ever had [apparently as rector of Keyston and Sevenoaks], being a thoughtful man, he took a walk in the churchyard, where the sexton was digging up a grave, and threw out a skull. The Doctor picked it up and turned it over in his hands. In so doing, he found a small sprigg, or headless nail, sticking in the temple, which he drew out secretly, and wrapped in the corner of his handkerchief. He then asked the grave-digger if he knew whose skull it was. The man said he did, declaring it belonged to a man who had kept a brandy-shop, an honest drunken fellow, who, one night taking two quarts of that comfortable substance, was found dead in his bed the next morning.

"Had he a wife?" asked the Doctor.

"Yes."

"Is she still living?"

"Yes."

"What character does she bear?"

"A very good one; only indeed the neighbors reflected on her, because she married the day after her husband was buried; though, to be sure, she had no great reason to grieve after him."

This was enough for the doctor, who, under the guise of visiting all of his parishioners, called on her. He asked her several questions, including what sickness her first husband had died of. She gave him the same account he had received from the Sexton. Donne suddenly opened the handkerchief and cried, in an authoritative voice, "Woman, do you know this nail?" She was struck with horror at the unexpected demand and instantly confessed.

- Laetitia Pilkington. *Memoirs of Mrs. Laetitia Pilkington, wife to the Rev. Mr. Matthew Pilkington; written by herself; wherein are occasionally interspersed all her poems with anecdotes of several eminent persons, living and dead.* Dublin; London: Printed and sold by R. Griffiths ... and G. Woodfall ... 1748-1754.

Doremus, Sarah (1802-1877). Never Alone.

Sarah Platt Doremus was a notable missions advocate and supporter.

ONE DAY a friend met Sarah Doremus at a Dwight L. Moody meeting in New York. Since Sarah seemed to be unaccompanied, she asked, "Are you here alone?"

"No, I am never alone," replied Sarah, who considered that God is always present.

- For more on Sarah Platt Doremus, see Edith Deen's *Great Women of the Christian Faith*. New York: Harper, 1956.

Dyneka, Peter (Twentieth Century). Tricked on His Voyage to America.

Born in 1898, Peter Dyneka came to America as a youth and was converted to Christ through the street ministry of Russian expatriates and the preaching of Paul Radar. He went on to become a dynamic evangelist to Russia and East Europe. One of his favorite sayings was, "Much prayer, much power; little prayer, little power."

PETER HAD NO IDEA how the world worked when he set sail for America. His mother packed black bread and onions for him to eat on the ship. He ate this all the way across, unable, he thought, to afford the meals in the dining room.

Some Russian sailors, playing on his ignorance, told him they'd slip him a little food if he'd help them with their work, so he pitched in, all the while envying the wealthier passengers, who could afford three square meals a day. Not until his last day aboard did he learn that meals were included in the price of his ticket. He often drew a parallel between this and the way many people try to work for the salvation Jesus has already purchased.

- Derived from Norman B. Rohrer and Peter Dyneka, Jr.'s *Peter Dynamite; twice born Russian*. Grand Rapids, Michigan: Baker Book House, 1975.

Elder Tu (fl. early Twentieth Century). The Case of the Stolen Banknotes.

Elder Tu was a prosperous Chinese businessman, short, kindly, full of determination, and also a man of deep faith—an intercessor who had dedicated himself to the welfare of local churches.

[Scott and some Chinese Christians, including Tu, had just finished a three-day series of meetings with prayer.] LIFTING OUR EYES to the horizon we saw a man running toward us. As he approached he gesticulated wildly. When near enough to make out who he was, we exclaimed, "Deacon Liu! What can be the matter?"

As he approached us he staggered. When he got to us he nearly dropped and could hardly speak for exhaustion. He was bathed in perspiration. We saw it was not all due to physical weariness. His beaded face showed anxiety, even terror. He gasped out, "Oh, I have lost it! I have lost it!" And sank to the ground. Then he moaned, "Stolen! Stolen!" We could hardly wait for him to get breath to give us his story.

Briefly it was this. Deacon Liu had been collecting an installment of the Chinese pastor's salary, then due; also partial payments on the wages of several school teachers and evangelists and Bible women, no small task, because this pastor presided over three churches, each in a different county, and extending through many villages. He had stopped in his own home overnight, expecting the next day to hunt out the parties concerned and pay them what was due...a small fortune in the local rural life...

To lose this money would be a calamity. On such salaries there was no margin to waste, yet that very night a thief had literally "dug through the wall" (as Jesus' illustration realistically puts it) and stolen the money, a roll of German bills (for Germany was then the master of "Kiautschou Kolonie," of which Tsingtao was the capital and seaport), and no money was then so desired as the German.

The deacon's first impulse had been to run to the magistrate, except there was little the authorities could or would do. Instead, he had hurried to us, a group of praying men and women, for comfort and aid.

None could doubt him. He was a tried collector and a carrier of church moneys of many years' standing, faithful as the daylight. Nevertheless, consternation reigned on the faces of all, all except Elder Tu...I could see that, while he was concerned and looked grave and sympathetic, he was not scared. Some of our group reminded me of a hen flopping with her head off, but not he.

Elder Tu illustrated in his life and conduct, almost as well as any individual I know, that state which Paul describes in Philippians 4:5, in which he exhorts his Christian friends to let their moderation be known unto all men. If that "moderation" means all the riches suggested in the Greek of balminess, of the yieldingness of selflessness in non-essentials, of sweet reasonableness, of mellowness of character, of spiritual poise and self-possession, then Elder Tu displayed "moderation" in this crisis.

That very morning we had studied together Isaiah 26:3. "You will keep him in perfect peace whose mind is fixed on You, because he trusts in You." This idea had sunk into him; rather, he had responded anew to it, as he had many times before in circumstances of perplexity and danger. Heathenism is an awful hell of worry and cussedness all the time anyway, and it is always troubling everybody upon whom it infringes. Elder Tu did not hope to escape out of it, but he knew he had a refuge in the midst of it.

At this juncture he spoke. "Shepherd Scott has to go on to his appointments. He cannot linger with us. He has his Holy Communion dates all set for his itinerary, and these are the most sacred of all engagements... He cannot turn aside to manage this affair. But he can pray as he journeys, and we will give ourselves to prayer here. This kind cometh not out but by prayer and fasting."

So we parted. Elder Tu went back to the village where he was a guest, betook himself to his Bible, to meditation and prayer, to praise and intercession. Thus he prayed for three days. Early the morning of the third day, as he was praying, just as the dawn was stealing over the earth, he heard a shout outside the wall and a slight rattle, as if a light package had dropped in the yard. Going to the door, he saw a paper roll before him at his feet. Picking it up, he noticed writing tied to it. It read as follows: "I could not keep it." Inside was the roll of German bills, intact.

• Adapted from Charles Ernest Scott's *Answered Prayer in China; some prayer-experiences of present-day Chinese Christians.* Philadelphia: The Sunday School Times Company, 1923.

Eliza P. (Nineteenth Century). The Infidel's Daughter.

All that we know about this young woman is this anecdote which was recorded by J. B. Finley.

WHEN TRAVELING the Cross Creek Circuit, in the year 1814, I witnessed one of the most wonderful manifestations of divine grace that has occurred within my personal knowledge—the conversion of an infidel, his wife, and only daughter. The daughter, whose name was Eliza, was beautiful and accomplished, having received a polite and fashionable education. The mother was an infidel like the father. The daughter, despite the cold and dreary sphere in which she had taken her existence and moved, was nevertheless of an amiable disposition. Although an infidel's daughter, and the child of a prayerless mother, she possessed a genial mind and a trusting heart. We have heard it said of some, "They are naturally religious," and if it were possible for any to have a native religious character, such might be ascribed to her. But, like the rich young ruler whom Jesus loved for the amiability of his disposition and the morality of his conduct, she lacked one thing, and that was the regenerating grace of God, without which all natural graces will prove unavailing as requisites for heaven.

At no very great distance from her father's residence there was a preaching-place, where the Methodist itinerants held meetings every fortnight. A special meeting had been appointed to continue several days, and as the father was absent at the legislature, she went without her mother's knowledge. Dressed as she was, in high fashion, when she entered the rude cabin and took her seat among the old-fashioned Methodists, she became an object of general attention. But she did not come out of mere idle curiosity; she was strangely drawn to the house of worship; there was a power at work of which she was unconscious. She had been taught that religion was a system of priestcraft; and though there might be some honest, deluded professors of religion, most of them were arrant hypocrites. She had never read the Bible, for her father considered it too immoral to put into her hands, preferring the writings of the French infidels, and even the blasphemies of Paine. Besides this, she had never heard a Gospel sermon. To her everything was new; and though she could appear with ease and grace in the drawing-room or gilded saloon, she felt embarrassed in the midst of a worshipping assembly. She composed herself however, as best she could; and when the preacher rose, and with solemn voice announced the text, "God so loved the world that He gave His Only Begotten Son, that whoever believes in Him should not perish, but have everlasting life," her attention was absorbed. This was the first Gospel message she ever heard, and it sounded strange to her ears. She had read Rousseau's opinion of Jesus Christ, and was disposed to look on him as an innocent, upright man, and she agreed with the philosopher in his opposition to other infidel writers who asserted that Jesus was an imposter. When the preacher fully opened his theme, representing God's love in sending his Son into the world to die for us, and the love of Christ in coming and taking upon Himself our load of guilt and shame, the young girl's heart was broken, and she wept aloud. Every eye was wet with tears, and many were the ardent prayers that went up to heaven in behalf of that weeping one.

When the meeting was over she went home; but so deeply was she affected by what she heard, that it was impossible for her to hide her feelings from her mother, who, in a stern voice, asked her where she had been, almost as soon as she entered the sitting room. On being informed that she had been to the meeting, the woman became much excited, and said, in an angry tone, "If you go again, those ignorant fanatics will ruin you forever; and if it comes to your father's ears that you have been to a Methodist meeting, he will banish you from the house; besides, you ought to know better. The instructions you have received should guard you against all such improprieties, and I hope hereafter I shall never hear of your being in such a place."

Night came on again, and with it the hour for meeting. Now commenced a conflict in the mind of the daughter. She had never disobeyed her mother, nor did she ever feel disposed to act contrary to her wishes in any respect; but her heart longed for the place of prayer, and she felt strongly drawn to it by an invisible agency she could hardly resist. "Shall I," said she to herself, "disobey my mother, and incur the displeasure of my father, and perhaps, banishment from home? But the preacher said that the Savior of the world declared that 'whosoever loves father and mother more than me, is not worthy of me; and whosoever will not forsake father and mother for my sake and the Gospel's shall not enter heaven.' I will forsake all for Christ."

She left home and went to meeting. At the close of the sermon, seekers were invited to kneel at the mourner's bench and pray for pardon. No sooner was the invitation given than Eliza pressed her way through the crowd, and fell upon the bench, crying for mercy. Her full heart now poured forth its grief, and sobs, and fervent prayers. The whole congregation was taken by surprise, and filled with utter astonishment, knowing, as most of them did, the utter contempt in which her father and mother held all religious exercises. Surely, they thought, this must be the special interposition of God; and every heart was lifted up in fervent prayer in her behalf. At that mourner's bench, Eliza struggled in agonizing prayer for two hours. It was midnight, and yet she was not converted. Never was mourner more deeply engaged. She had made the last resolve. One after another of the faithful had poured out their hearts at the mercy-seat in her behalf; hymn after hymn was sung, as only those can sing who sing with the spirit; but still she came not through the dark valley. Faith began to flag and some thought the penitent must disrobe herself of her hat and plume, and flowers and ruffles, before the Lord could bless. But God looks at the heart, and he saw, in its deep recesses, a soul absorbed in grief, conscious of nothing but its own guilt and sin. At length the last hymn was rolling up from swelling hearts and tuneful voices to heaven. The last stanza was reached and as the last strain sounded in the ear of the penitent, she gently threw back her head, and opened calm blue eyes, sparkling with tears—the tears of sins forgiven. She arose and embraced the sisters who had prayed with her, and pointed her to the Lamb of God who takes away the sin of the world. She had passed many a late night in scenes of mirth and revelry, but never did such joy and gladness come to her heart as she experienced on that occasion. She returned home, feeling now that she could gladly bear anything for the sake of her Lord and Master.

When she arrived she related to her mother what had occurred, and exclaimed, "Oh, how precious is the Savior!" She would have embraced her mother, but she repulsed her, and reproached her, telling her that if she did not cease this nonsense, she would drive her away from the house, and that she had disgraced herself and ruined herself forever. Eliza retired to her room, and spent the remainder of the night in prayer and praise to God.

Soon it was noised about that the infidel's daughter was converted; and some friends, supposing that they would render him a service, wrote to him, giving him the most absurd and ridiculous accounts of her behavior while at the mourner's bench, and after she was converted. When Mr. P. received the intelligence he was greatly enraged, and swore that he would banish his daughter from his house, and disinherit and disown her. But all this did not sway the daughter; for she realized the truth of the divine declaration, "When my father and mother forsake me, then the Lord will take me up."

The day was at length fixed for her father's return home, and the daughter placed herself at the window to watch for his arrival. In the afternoon she saw him approaching on horseback, and hurried to the gate to meet him. With a pale, sweet countenance she stepped forward to hug and kiss him; but he rudely seized her by the arm, and horsewhipped her out the gate, telling her to be gone, and, with many curses, forebade her to return. She went weeping down the lane, but thought what her Savior had suffered for her, and her heart was steadied under its pain. She realized then, to its full extent, what it was to love the Lord Jesus more than all else.

Not far from her father's residence lived a godly Methodist, a poor widow, and she was aware of the state of affairs at the house of Mr. P. When she saw Eliza coming toward her that evening, she could guess why. The poor widow gave the girl a cordial reception, and offered words of kindness and comfort. Eliza asked permission to go to the little room, and to remain there undisturbed. No sooner was she alone than she fell upon her knees and commenced pouring out her soul to God in prayer for her unconverted father and mother.

But we must return to the father. As he gazed after Eliza, sobbing as she went down the lane, it seemed as though a thousand fiends of darkness had taken possession of his soul. He went to the house and met his wife, but she was equally wretched, having witnessed what was done. He sat down. They spoke in monosyllables. The supper hour arrived, but he refused to eat, though he had ridden all day. He went to the library and turned over his books and papers, but it was in a hurried manner, and with a vacant look. He went to his bedroom, but not to rest, for sleep departed from his eyes. Next day he wandered about over his farm and through the woods, like one seeking for something lost. The cause of his trouble his proud heart would not allow him to admit. Unable to find rest, he again sought his bedroom; but his anguish increased, and he began to see the shallowness of his infidelity, and also its dark, horrid nature, in that it could prompt him to drive his lovely and otherwise obedient daughter from his house, simply because she had become a Christian. From that moment he was a changed man; from a hard impenitent sinner he was brought to relent and pray; and he continued for hours. Present to the eye of his mind was the image of his banished Eliza.

He rose and sent for her, and again returned to prayer. He got up again and walked in the garden, and there, beneath Eliza's favorite bower, he knelt down, and again lifted up his heart to God in prayer. At length the deep, dark, dense cloud broke away, and the Sun of Righteousness arose and beamed upon him, and lighted up his almost distracted mind with the peace and calm of heaven.

For 24 hours, without eating or sleeping, Eliza remained in the widow's room, engaged in earnest supplication for her father. The widow, looking out the window, saw the servant coming with two horses, and running into the little room exclaimed, "Eliza, your father has sent for you."

The happy child arose, and soon was at the gate from which she had been driven the night before, a fugitive and alone. She saw her weeping father coming to meet her, and instantly jumping down, sprang into his arms, and he embraced her with a love he had never felt before.

"My angel of mercy," said he, "I give you my heart and my hand to travel with you to the heavenly inheritance." It was a happy meeting. The mother soon joined the father and daughter in the service of God; and they continued faithful disciples of Christ, till they were called from the church militant on earth to the Church triumphant in heaven.

- Adapted from an account by J. B. Finley; quoted in George Coles' *Heroines of Methodism.* New York: Carlton & Lanahan, 1869.

Elliot, Jim (1927-1956). Two Close Calls.

Jim Elliot was a missionary martyr in Ecuador.

YEARS BEFORE JIM ELLIOT MET MARTYRDOM in Ecuador with four other missionaries, he had ceased to think his life belonged to himself. Among his reasons for this were two close calls in which he could easily have been killed.

In the first, while hunting, a friend accidentally discharged his gun while trying to climb over a barbed wire fence, and the bullet cut through Jim's hair. In the second incident, Jim and some buddies stalled on a railroad track. They scrambled from the car seconds before an onrushing train smashed it to smithereens.

Jim wrote to his parents after the second incident, "It sobered me considerably to think that the Lord kept me from harm in this. Certainly He has a work that He wants me in somewhere."

- Derived from Elisabeth Elliot's *Shadow of the Almighty; The Life and Testament of Jim Elliot.* New York: Harper and Brothers, 1958.

Erasmus (1467-1536). Mistaken for a Physician.

Erasmus would spend his life in continual danger, and not just for his religious views. Had he been killed in either incident related in this anecdote, his greatest works would never have been written.

A SINGULAR ADVENTURE Erasmus met with in Bologna in 1507, throws light upon the customs of the time. During plague it was the custom of the physicians to wear a white sash across the shoulder down the breast and back, so that they could be readily distinguished and avoided. They also usually passed along deserted streets, as otherwise they would be stoned! According to the French use, Erasmus carried a kind of white band on his monk's vestment. At one time two roughs saw him, and were about to attack him sword in hand, though a woman told them that the band indicated an Augustinian priest and not a physician. But they would not desist, and would have played him an ugly trick if he had not escaped to a friend's house.

At another time a crowd surrounded him, armed with stones and sticks, crying out, "Kill the dog, kill the dog!" A priest passed, and whispered to Erasmus, "The asses!" but did not disperse the crowd or explain their mistake to them. Soon a young man of fine dress came out of a neighboring house, to whom Erasmus went as to a savior, told him he did not know the language of the country, and did not know what they wanted of him. "Be sure," responded the Bolognese, "that if you do not take off this piece of cloth, they will stone you every day." So Erasmus divested himself of this mark of the Augustinian order, and obtained from the pope a permission to appear in regular clerical garb, without monastic trappings, or a costume half-clerical, half-lay.

- John Alfred Faulkner. *Erasmus: the Scholar.* Cincinnati, Ohio: Jennings and Graham, 1907.

Escapes (Various Dates). Miscellaneous Escapes.

John Calvin was a Reformer in Geneva, famed for his theology. Hugo Grotius was an Arminian imprisoned by Calvinists in the Netherlands.

CHRISTIANS, BY SPEAKING GOD'S WORD faithfully, have often stirred up Satanic opposition. Some have been imprisoned or otherwise fallen into desperate danger from which they have had to escape. The New Testament gives at least three examples of escapes. In the first, outraged listeners seized Jesus and dragged him to the edge of a cliff to hurl him over. It is not clear how he escaped, for scripture only says he walked out of their midst. Later Peter was freed from prison by an angel and Paul was lowered in a basket over the city wall at Damascus.

During the Reformation, Calvin escaped from Paris by climbing down a rope made from sheets and then fled, disguised as a farmer with a hoe over his shoulder. The Christian lawyer and scholar Hugo Grotius escaped prison through the faithfulness of his wife and the wit of a maid; the wife hid him in a book box and the maid conducted it to safety. When the carriers complained that the box was heavy enough to contain the man rather than his books, she deflected suspicion by the pert reply, "You know how heavy those Arminian books are."

Eusebius of Samosata (died ca. 380). Fearless Reply.

Bishop Eusebius, a firm opponent of Arianism (which denies the full divinity of Christ), signed the Nicene creed. Through a messenger, the Arian emperor Constantius threatened to cut off Eusebius right hand if he did not surrender a certain document. Eusebius presented both hands saying "Strike them both off. I will not surrender the document by which the injustice of the Arians can be proved." He died from being struck on the head by a roof tile flung by an Arian woman.

WHEN VALENS, THE EMPEROR, sent messengers to seduce Eusebius to heresy by fair words and large promises, he answered, "Sirs, these speeches are fit to catch little children; but we, who are taught and nourished by the holy scriptures, are ready to suffer a thousand deaths, rather than permit one tittle of the Scriptures to be altered."

Subsequently the emperor threatened to confiscate his goods, to torment, to banish, or to kill him, he answered, "He needs not fear confiscation, who has nothing to lose; nor banishment, to whom heaven alone is a country; nor torments, whose body will be destroyed at one blow; nor death, which is the only way to set him at liberty from sin and sorrow."

- Adapted from Walter Baxendale's *Dictionary of Anecdote, Incident, Illustrative Fact*. New York: Thomas Whittaker, 1889.

Eveillan, M. (Undated). No Carpet.

Angers is a French City, the capital of the department of Maine el Loire.

M. EVEILLAN, formerly Archdeacon of Angers, was noted for his humane and charitable disposition towards the poor. On one occasion, when a friend expressed surprise that none of his rooms were carpeted, he replied, "When I enter my house in the winter, I do not hear any complaints of cold from the furniture of my rooms; but the poor who stand shivering at my doors tell me but too plainly that they have need of clothing."

- *The Book of Three Hundred Anecdotes Historical, Literary, and Humorous—A New Selection*. London and New York: Burns & Oates, n.d.

Faraday, Michael (1791-1867). Appearances Can Be Deceiving; Heavenly Occupations.

Born into an impoverished home, Michael Faraday made the best use of his opportunities to became a notable scientist, famed for his chemical researches and discoveries in electromagnetism. At the same time, he was a devout Christian, whose faith prevented him from weapons research—and also kept him transparent and humble.

Dirty tubes. ONCE WHEN PERFORMING an experiment with chlorine before Dr. Paris (friend and biographer of Faraday's mentor, Sir Humphrey Davy), Faraday obtained a liquid which had an oily appearance.

Dr. Paris chided Faraday, assuming the oil was from a negligent use of dirty tubes. Although this was not true, Faraday patiently bore the rebuke. However, he had trained himself always to examine unexpected results, and the next day he was able to send this triumphant note to Dr. Paris,

Dear Sir,
    The oil you noticed yesterday turns out to be liquid chlorine.
                              Yours faithfully,
                              M. Faraday.

- This incident is mentioned in most biographies of Michael Faraday, including L. Pearce Williams' *Michael Faraday; a biography*. Simon and Schuster, 1971.

"I shall be with Christ." FARADAY WAS ONCE ASKED "Have you conceived to yourself what will be your occupation in the next world?"

Pausing a moment to find the right words, Faraday replied with a quotation from Paul, "Eye hath not seen, nor ear heard, neither have entered into the heart of men, the things which God has prepared for them that love him. I shall be with Christ, and that's enough."

- Adapted from Walter Baxendale's *Dictionary of Anecdote, Incident, Illustrative Fact.* New York: Thomas Whittaker, 1889.

Fawcett, John (1740-1817). Forget Moving.

Dr. John Fawcett was the pastor of a small Baptist church at Wainsgate, England.

CALLED FROM WAINSGATE to a larger church in London in 1772, John Fawcett accepted. His small church could not fully support him. So he preached his farewell sermon, and loaded his books, furniture, and household items into wagons. All was ready for departure, but his parishioners gathered around him, and with tears in their eyes begged him to stay.

His wife said, "Oh John, John, I cannot bear this."

"Neither can I," exclaimed the good pastor, "and we will not go. Unload the wagons and put everything as it was before."

His decision was hailed with great joy by his people, and he wrote the hymn we know as "Blest Be the Tie that Binds" in commemoration of the event. To supplement his income, he took pupils.

- This story is told in a number of books, including Ira D. Sankey's *My Life and the Story of the Gospel Hymns*. Philadelphia: Sunday School Times, 1907.

Fénelon, François (1651-1715). Passionate Pupil; Palace Burns; Empty Chapel.

François Fénelon was a French Catholic mystic known for his self-control, faith, gentle spirit, and love. A pioneer in educational techniques, it was he that Louis XIV selected to train his grandson, the Duke of Burgundy, a passionate and somewhat deranged child. It was a weighty responsibility and required all Fénelon's immense understanding of human nature. The Duke learned to love and respect him above all other men. After Louis turned against Fénelon, the Duke, then a young man, was forbidden to visit him. In 1702, however, the king relented and said the Duke might meet Fénelon, but only in public. At that meeting, in a loud voice, audible to all in the room the Duke exclaimed, "I am sensible my Lord Archbishop, what I owe to you, and you know what I am." Those words hearkened back to a crucial episode many years earlier, the subject of this first anecdote.

A passionate pupil. ONCE, HOWEVER, there was a serious scene between Fénelon and the duke, which appears to have had a lasting influence upon the prince. Fénelon had been obliged to reprove him with more than usual severity, and the boy, in angry pride, had resisted, exclaiming, "No, no, sir; I remember who I am, and who you are." It was impossible to pass over such a speech and maintain authority; but acting upon his own maxim, never to administer reproof while either person concerned is excited, Fénelon made no reply, and for the remainder of the day preserved a total silence toward his pupil, who could not fail to perceive by his manner that the usually indulgent master was much displeased. Night came with no explanation.

But the next morning, as soon as the prince was awake, the abbé came into his room, and, addressing him in a grave, ceremonious manner, very unlike the easy tone of their usual exchanges, said: "I do not know, Monsieur, whether you remember what you said to me yesterday, that you knew what you are and what I am; but it is my duty to teach you your ignorance alike of both. You fancy yourself a greater personage than I—some of your servants may have told you so; but since you oblige me to do it I must tell you that I am greater than you. You must see at once that there can be no question of birth in the matter. It is one of personal merit. You can have no doubt that I am your superior in understanding and knowledge; you know nothing but what I have taught you, and that is a mere shadow compared with what you have yet to learn. As to authority, you have none over me, whereas I, on the other hand, have full and entire authority over you, as the king has often told you. Perhaps you imagine that I think myself fortunate in holding the office I fill about yourself; but there again you are mistaken. I undertook it only to obey the king, and in no way for the irksome privilege of being your preceptor. And to convince you of this truth I am now going to take you to his majesty and beg of him to appoint someone else whose care of you, I hope, will be more successful than mine."

This was no idle threat; for Fénelon had always been determined to resign the tutorship as soon as he felt himself to be failing in it; and the prince was obliged to weigh his pride against his love. His love proved the greater; for life had been very different for him since Fénelon came into it, and no sacrifice of his vanity was too galling if he might cancel his offense and keep his friend. Moreover, he was sensitive to the last degree to public opinion and the faintest shadow of disgrace. What would the world think of a prince who was so hopelessly naughty that a man so universally admired and respected was forced to give him up, and what would become of the poor little boy to whom his nearest relatives were after all, only "His Majesty" and "Monseigneur," if the dear, kind preceptor, who loved him and devoted himself entirely to him, were to go away? Poor Louis!

The storm broke out anew; but this time it was of penitence and shame, while with passionate sobs and tears he cried out: "O Monsieur, I am sorry for what I did yesterday. If you tell the king he will not care for me anymore; and what will people think if you leave me? I promise, O I promise ever so much, that you shall not have to complain of me if only you will promise not to go."

But Fénelon would promise nothing—the lesson would be lost if it were not sharp—and for a whole day he allowed the duke to undergo the pangs of anxiety and uncertainty. But at last, when his repentance seemed unlikely to be soon forgotten, Madame de Maintenon's intercession was admitted, and the preceptor consented to remain.

- Adapted from James Mudge's *Fénelon: the Mystic*. Cincinnati: Jennings and Graham, 1906.

His palace burns. THE VENERABLE ARCHBISHOP of Cambray, whose humanity was unbounded, was in the constant habit of visiting the cottages of the peasants, and administering consolation and relief in their distress. When they were driven from their habitations by the alarms of war, he received them into his house, and served them at his table. During the war, his house was always open to the sick and wounded, whom he lodged and provided with every necessity for their relief. Besides his constant hospitality to the military, he performed a most munificent act of patriotism and humanity after the disastrous winter of 1709 (which killed 3.5% of the French population), by opening his granaries and distributing gratuitously corn to the value of 100,000 livres [at a time when an unskilled worker in Paris might earn less than 300 livres a year]. And when his palace at Cambray, and all his books and furniture, were destroyed by fire, he bore it with the utmost firmness, saying, "It is better all these should be burned, than the cottage of one poor family."

- *The Book of Three Hundred Anecdotes Historical, Literary, and Humorous—A New Selection.* London and New York: Burns & Oates, n.d.

Empty chapel. AT ANOTHER TIME king Louis XIV was astonished to find only Fénelon and the priest at the chapel, instead of a numerous congregation as usual. "What is the reason of this?" asked the king.

"Why," replied Fénelon, "I caused it to be given out, Sire, that your majesty did not attend chapel today, so that you might know who came to worship God, and who to flatter the king."

- Adapted from Sholto and Reuben Percy. *The Percy Anecdotes.* Harper & Brothers, 1847.

Finney, Charles (1792-1875). A Typical Revival.

Charles Finney was an American revival leader who insisted that responsibility for conversion rests with ourselves, and that revival leaders, while relying on the Holy Spirit, must use the means God has provided for soul-winning. Humans have free will and the ability to act and must use both. This teaching met much opposition, but he had great success in winning furious antagonists to Christ, even in areas where churchgoers themselves were hardened to Gospel appeals. Critics denounced his theology (which, indeed, walked dangerously close to heresy) and his methods (which, in any hands other than those of a Spirit-filled, loving evangelist, can be hurtful); to which he responded, "Show me the fruits of your ministry, and if they so far exceed mine as to give me evidence that you have found a more excellent way, I will adopt your views. But do you expect me to abandon my views and practices when the results justify my methods?"

A YOUNG LADY from Stephantown came to New Lebanon and heard Finney. She was so impressed that she invited him to come to her place and preach. Finney told her his hands were full, and he thought he could not. Her response was choked with deep feeling, and Finney became stirred profoundly over the condition of the place. It seems that the town's only place of worship was a run down Presbyterian Church whose minister had become an infidel...Nearly the whole town was in a state of impenitence. Most of the people lived scattered along a street nearly five miles long, and there was not a religious family on that street, nor a single house in which family prayer was maintained.

Finney made an appointment to preach the next Sunday. Here occurred one of the characteristic incidents of which Finney's life was so full. He asked the person who was to take him in his carriage, "Have you a steady horse?"

"Oh yes!" he replied; "perfectly so. What made you ask that question?"

"Because," said Finney, "if the Lord wants me to go to Stephentown, the devil will prevent it if he can; and if you have not a steady horse, he will try to make him kill me." Strange to say, the horse ran away twice, a thing which he had never done before, and almost killed them.

The people were solemn and attentive. Miss S--- spent the whole of the following night in prayer. The spirit of prayer also came powerfully upon Finney and others. Soon the Word of God brought the strongest men down and rendered them entirely helpless.

On the evening of the day of a State election, one of the men who had sat at the table to receive votes all day was so overcome by conviction that he could not leave his seat. In another pew another man was in the same condition. The infidel preacher strenuously opposed the work, but God struck him down, so that during the revival he died a horrible death. It broke the spell of his influence, and there was a great turning to the Lord. There was one family of sixteen, and another of seventeen, all of whom were converted. The revival was characterized by a mighty spirit of prevailing prayer, overwhelming conviction of sin, sudden and powerful conversions to Christ, great love and abounding joy of among the converts, and much earnestness, activity, and usefulness in their prayers and labors for others. Nearly all the inhabitants of the town were gathered into the church, and the town was morally renovated.

- Adapted from A. M. Hills. *Life of Charles G. Finney*. Cincinatti, Ohio: Office of God's Revivalist, 1902.

Fisher, John (ca. 1469-1535). Seeks Bible Comfort.

John Fisher, a staunch Roman Catholic, and the Vice-Chancellor of Cambridge, was ardent to win souls and to educate the clergy of England. He brought Erasmus to England. Later, he fell into disfavor with Henry VIII for not supporting the king's projected divorce. He died for privately rejecting Henry VIII's claim to head the English church.

WHEN DR. FISHER, Bishop of Rochester, who was cruelly condemned by Henry VIII, came out of the Tower of London and saw the scaffold, he took out of his pocket a Greek New Testament, and looking up at heaven, he exclaimed, "Now, O Lord, direct me to some passage which may support me through this awful scene." He opened the book, and his eye glanced on the text, "This is life eternal, to know You, the only true God, and Jesus Christ, whom You have sent." The bishop instantly closed the book, and said, "Praised be the Lord! This is sufficient both for me and for eternity."

- Adapted from Walter Baxendale's *Dictionary of Anecdote, Incident, Illustrative Fact*. New York: Thomas Whittaker, 1889.

Forsyth, Christina (1844-ca. 1917). God's Protection.

Widowed shortly after her marriage, Christina Forsyth asked for and received one of the most difficult mission assignments in Southern Africa—Xolobe, a field which others had abandoned as hopeless. God favored her endeavors, granting her many souls and protecting her life.

ONE SUNDAY she had been attending communion at Paterson and was detained; it was five o'clock in the afternoon before she set out to trudge the ten miles back. Darkness fell but she kept on. At last she lost the roughly-defined track and went wandering amongst the rocks and scrub. It was impossible to tell where she was, and she abandoned the attempt to proceed and took shelter for the night behind a boulder. The hours passed slowly; she wearied for the dawn. With the light she discovered that she was resting on the edge of a precipice. One step more and she would have been killed.

She tramped to Xolobe and took up her duties as if nothing had happened.

- Adapted from W. P. Livingstone's *Christina Forsyth of Fingoland*. New York: George H. Dolan Co., 1919.

Fox, George (1624-1690). The Incident that Drove Him to Seek God.

Eminent as the founder of the Quakers, George Fox was a noble and persuasive man, who suffered much for his beliefs. Here is his account of the incident which brought him to a spiritual crisis and set him on the intense quest after God from which he emerged with the understanding that he must rely upon the inner light God gave him (which in his case included much memorized Scripture), and on nothing else.

WHEN I APPROACHED NINETEEN years of age, I had some business at a fair. One of my cousins, whose name was Bradford, and who professed to be a Christian was there with another professed Christian and came over to invite me to drink part of a jug of beer with them. Being thirsty, I went in with them, for I loved anyone that had a sense of good, or who sought after the Lord. But after we had drunk a glass each, they began to drink healths and called for more drink, agreeing that whoever first refused a drink should pay for the rest. I was saddened that anyone who made a profession of religion should behave like this. They pained me very much, for never before had anyone (least of all professing Christians) made such a suggestion to me.

Consequently, I rose to leave, and putting my hand in my pocket took out a coin and laid it on the table in front of them, saying, "If that's how its going to be, I'm leaving." So I left; and when I had taken care of my business, I went home, but did not go to bed that night and could not sleep, but sometimes walked up and down, and sometimes prayed and cried to the Lord, who said unto me, "You see how young people join together in foolish behavior and old people in worldliness; but you must leave them all, both young and old, and distance yourself from their affairs, and be like a stranger to everyone."

Then at the command of God on the 9th of September,* 1643, I left my relations and broke off all close association with young or old...

*Being a Quaker, George Fox used the number of the month rather than the pagan-derived name. At that time, the year was reckoned from March 1st in England, so he called September the Seventh month.

• Modernized from George Fox's *Journal*. 1694.

French Priests in the Revolution. (ca. 1795). The Gendarmes and a Priest; A Forgiving Priest.

The French Revolution, which ran from 1789 to 1799, sometimes seemed to embrace Catholicism and at other times violently persecuted priests, monks, and nuns.

The Gendarmes and the Priest. DURING THE FRENCH REVOLUTION a priest took refuge in the house of a farmer. Some gendarmes having heard of it came to the house one evening. The whole family were gathered round the hearth, and among them was the priest, disguised as a servant. When the soldiers entered everyone grew pale; the soldiers asked the farmer if there was not a priest concealed in the house.

"Gentlemen," returned he, without losing his presence of mind, "you see very well there is no priest here; but one might conceal himself in the house without my knowledge; so I will not prevent you from doing your duty; search the house from cellar to garret." Then he said to the priest, "I say, Jacques, take your lantern and show these gentlemen everywhere; let them see every corner of the farm."

The gendarmes made a minute inspection of the house, uttering many curses and threats against the priest, promising themselves to pay him well for the trouble he had cost them, if they found him. Seeing their search was useless, they prepared to leave.

As they were going the farmer said, "Pray gentlemen, remember the boy." They gave the disguised priest a small tip, and, thanking him for his civility, took their leave.

- *The Book of Three Hundred Anecdotes Historical, Literary, and Humorous—A New Selection.* London and New York: Burns & Oates, n.d.

The Forgiving French Priest. THE INHABITANTS OF A VILLAGE in Dauphine had determined to sacrifice their lord to their vengeance during the Revolution, and were only dissuaded from it by the eloquence of the curé, who thus addressed them: "My friends," said he, "the day of vengeance is arrived; the individual who has so long tyrannized over you must now suffer his merited punishment. As the care of this flock has been entrusted to me, it is appropriate and necessary for me to watch over their best interests, nor will I forsake their righteous cause. Suffer me only to be your leader, and swear to me that in all circumstances you will follow my example."

All the villagers swore they would.

"And," continued he, "you will further solemnly promise to enter into any engagement which I may now make, and to remain faithful to this your oath."

All the villagers exclaimed, "We do."

"Well then," said he, solemnly taking the oath, "I swear to forgive our lord."

Unexpected as this was, the villagers kept their word and forgave him.

- *The Book of Three Hundred Anecdotes Historical, Literary, and Humorous—A New Selection.* London and New York: Burns & Oates, n.d.

Gaddis, Maxwell Pierson (1811-1888). Reporting Christ's Non-Appearance at the Millerite Tabernacle.

Methodist evangelist, Maxwell Pierson Gaddis provided this eyewitness report of the day Christ did not fulfill William Miller's calculations and return to earth.

AS I HAD HAD CONSIDERABLE TROUBLE with some of the [Millerites] in my congregation, I concluded to go down to Cincinnati and witness for myself the finale of this wide-spreading delusion. I arrived there in good time, but was told that the house was so full I could not get in. They spent the night in "watching for their Lord;" but he did not appear. The next morning I was informed they were still "robed," and at the tabernacle, wondering why he "delayed his coming." I met Judge Johnston, and we agreed to go down in company at nine o'clock. On our arrival there we found the house still about two-thirds full. Some were standing, and others walking about, distributing a paper headed the "Last Warning." At times they would sing a beautiful hymn. About twelve o'clock they became exceedingly restless and some started to leave.

Then an old veteran, called Deacon Smith, arose and remarked, with a strong voice, "Brethren and sisters, we have now arrived at the Red Sea. I exhort you, one and all, to stand still and see the salvation of God!" Then, pulling out his watch to note the time, he said, "My faith is unwavering; the time is not up yet by more than one hour." This speech was followed by many hearty responses, and one or two Millerite songs. A Mr. H. next arose and said, "If Christ does not come this day I will believe this Bible false!" clapping his hands violently on the word of God before him. A sister then spoke incoherently for a considerable time, clearly evincing that her mind had lost its proper balance. When she was done speaking, another lady with whom I was well acquainted, arose to "show us her opinion," and wound up some very foolish and common-place remarks by saying, "that she knew this was the time for Christ's second coming, for when she got up on yesterday morning she saw red streaks in the sky toward the east." This was one of the ablest arguments offered on that occasion.

About one o'clock, Rev. Deacon W. arose and spoke substantially as follows: "I never did fix upon the precise time myself, and I always told my brethren they would get into trouble if they did; but they would not listen to me, but followed other leaders. My faith is this: I believe that at this period the 'sign of the

Son of man will appear in heaven,'" but how much longer after the appearance of the "sign of the Son of man," before the Son of man would actually appear, he could not inform them; but said, "Brethren, as this is a Jewish reckoning, made for the land of Palestine, there must be some allowance made for 'latitude and longitude' when time is reckoned; but I tell you I believe the most important thing after all is, to be ready; and now I want you all to pray that your old friend J. W. may not be like some 'balloon ascensions' that I have witnessed in this city, which, after going up for a time, fall suddenly to the earth again; but when I do begin to ascend I hope I may keep on till I enter the portals of paradise." This address was followed by hearty responses from the Adventists and laughter among the spectators.

- Maxwell Pierson Gaddis. *Footprints of an Itinerant.* Cincinnati, Ohio: Methodist Book Concern, 1855.

Roman Games. (ca. 70-ca. 317). Christian Witness in the Games.

One of the more horrific aspects of Roman civilization was its brutal games, which wantonly disregarded human life by presenting torture and killings as public entertainment.

CHRISTIANS THROUGHOUT THE ROMAN EMPIRE attended the games, brutal as they were, although leaders such as Tertullian exhorted them not to. Many went to the executions anyhow, partly to support fellow-Christians, who were among those being killed, and partly to equip themselves to be witnesses in their turn. According to a letter written by Montanus, they hoped to learn to die bravely for the faith. Those Christians who perished in the arena preached to the crowds and called on fellow Christians to be steadfast witnesses. They endeavored to show a brave and cheerful face during their ordeal, setting a good example.

- Joyce E. Salisbury documents this in her book *Perpetua's Passion; the death and memory of a young Roman woman.* New York: Routledge, 1997.

Gardeau, Father (Undated Episode). Blush, Ladies.

I have no information about Father Gardeau beyond this.

FATHER GARDEAU WAS DISPLEASED that his words against immodesty produced little effect among the women of his congregation, who persisted in the prevailing fashion of the day, of displaying their uncovered bosoms; so he exclaimed during a sermon: "Cover your nakedness! at least before me. Is it necessary to tell you, that I am made of flesh and blood, as other men?"

At this everyone laughed; particularly the ladies.

He then assumed his grave tone. "When I speak to you with cautious decency, and ambiguous expressions, you are deaf; and when I address you in the clearest ones, you find them ridiculous, and you laugh. What hope can there remain of your amendment?"

- Adapted from Isaac D'Israeli's *Curiosities of Literature.* London: Frederick and Warne, 1881.

Geneva Nuns (1532). Bewildered.

The anecdote that follows, which took place when Farel brought Reformation to Geneva, leads the reflective reader to two considerations: one, what a pity that human lives were so wasted behind cloister walls and rendered incapable of practical action; and two, how great a disruption the Reformation was for many.

THE PRIESTS AND NUNS gradually took their departure. The sprightly Jeanne de Jussie tells of the going to Annecy: "It was a piteous thing to see this holy company in such a plight, so overcome with fatigue and grief that several swooned by the way. It was rainy weather, and all were compelled to walk through muddy roads, except four poor invalids who were in a carriage. There were six poor old women who had taken their vows more than sixty years before. Two of these, who were past sixty-six, and had never seen anything of the world, fainted away repeatedly. They could not bear the wind; and when they saw the cattle in the fields, they took the cows for bears, and the long-wooled sheep for ravening wolves." It took the nuns from five in the morning until near midnight to go a short league [about three miles] to Annecy.

- Richard Taylor Stevenson. *John Calvin: the Statesman.* Cincinnati, Ohio; Jennings and Graham, 1907.

George III (1738-1820). Proper Subject of Praise.

George III, the British king against whom the United States revolted, suffered bouts of insanity, probably owing to porphyria, a disorder in which cells fail to make the hemes that give blood their color. George, however, was a Christian. The following anecdote

shows him more sane than many a "normal"person.

ONE OF THE FIRST ACTS performed by George III, after his accession to the throne, was to issue an order prohibiting any of the clergy who should be called to preach before him from paying him any compliment in their discourses. His Majesty was led to this from the fulsome adulation which Dr. Thomas Wilson, prebendary of Westminster, thought proper to deliver in the Chapel-Royal. Instead of thanks, Wilson received from his royal auditor a pointed reprimand, his Majesty observing, "I came to chapel to hear the praises of God, not my own."

- Adapted from Walter Baxendale's *Dictionary of Anecdote, Incident, Illustrative Fact*. New York: Thomas Whittaker, 1889.

Gilmour, James (1843-1891). Unusual Marriage Made in Heaven.

If anything can be said of James Gilmour it was that he was unconventional and forthright. This was as true of him in his youth, when he roamed the hills of Scotland alone or boldly confronted his friends and acquaintances about sin and salvation, as it was in his maturity, when he wandered Mongolia alone. His proposal of marriage, from China, by letter, to a girl he had never met, would also seem odd were there not a good deal of faith and heavenly guidance in it as the following excerpts show. And Emily Prankard's photograph shows she was a lovely woman that any lonely man might imagine himself in love with.

DURING THE YEAR 1873 James Gilmour devoted much thought to the question of marriage. Unusual as he was, in so many ways, it was to be expected that in this great undertaking he would depart from ordinary methods. In 1872 Rev. S. E. Meech married a Miss Prankard, of London. In 1873, James Gilmour boarded with Rev. and Mrs. Meech. There he saw a portrait of Mrs. Meech's sister, and often heard her referred to in conversation. Towards the close of 1873, he took Mrs. Meech into his confidence, and asked permission to correspond with her sister.

Emily Prankard accepted Gilmour after receiving his first letter, which was a proposal of marriage, and she visited his family in Scotland. He wrote his folks about it.

"You have seen Miss Prankard, but you have not told me what you think of her. She was delighted with her visit to Scotland and with you all. You will be glad to hear that I have had some delightful letters from her. I wrote her, and she has written me in the most unrestrained way concerning her spiritual hopes and condition, and though we have never seen each other, yet we know more of each other's inmost life and soul than, I am quite certain, most lovers know of each other even after long personal courtship. It is quite delightful to think that even now we can talk by letter with perfect unreserve, and I tell you this because I know you will be glad to hear it. I knew she was a pious girl, else I would not have asked her to come out to be a missionary's wife, but she turns out better even than I thought, and I am not much afraid as to how we shall get on together."

After the wedding, he wrote good-humoredly to a friend whose serious warning against taking an English wife had come too late. It revealed more fully the faith principles he had followed in obtaining his bride.

"My dear _____, Your kind, long, and much-looked-for letter dated May 12, 1873, and August 21, 1874, reached me on January 9, 1875. Many thanks for it, but I think it would be quite as well in future to send me half the quantity in half the time, if you really find you cannot write me oftener. As I was married on December 8, 1874, to Mrs. Meech's sister, that lady, Mrs. Gilmour, had the great pleasure of reading your earnest, long, and reiterated warning to me not to have her. Your warning came too late. Had you posted your letter on May 12, 1873, it might have been in time, as the first letter that opened our [his and Emily's] acquaintance was written in January 1874. If nothing else will have effect with you, perhaps the thought that you might have saved me from the fate of having an English wife may have some effect in moving you to post your letters early, even though they should not be so long and full.

"About my wife: as I want you to know her, I introduce you to her. She is a jolly girl, as much, perhaps more, of a Christian and a Christian missionary than I am. I don't know whether I told you how it came about. I proposed first to a Scotch girl, but found I was too late; I then put myself and the direction of this affair—I mean the finding of a wife—into God's hands, asking Him to look me out one, a good one too, and very soon I found myself in a position to propose to Miss Prankard with all reasonable evidence that she was the right sort of girl, and with some hope that she would not disdain the offer. We had never seen each other, and had never corresponded, but she had heard much about me from people in England who knew me, and I had heard a good deal of her and seen her letters written to her sister and to her sister's husband. The first letter I wrote her was to propose, and the first letter she wrote to me was to accept—romantic enough!

"I proposed in January, went up to Mongolia in spring, rode about on my camels till July, and came down to Kalgan to find that I was an accepted man! I went to Tientsin to meet her; we arrived here on Thursday, and were married on Tuesday morning. We had a quiet week, then I went to the country on a nine days' tour, and came back two days before Christmas. We have been at home ever since. Such is the romance of a matter-of-fact man.

"You will see that the whole thing was gone about simply on the faith principle, and from its success I am inclined to think more and more highly of the plan. Without any gammon, I am much more happy than ever even in my day-dreams I ventured to imagine I might be. It is not only me that my wife pleases, but she has gained golden opinions from most of the people who have met her among my friends and acquaintances in Scotland and China. My parents were scared one day last year by receiving a letter from a lady in England, a lady whose name they had not known before, stating that her daughter had decided to become my wife. Didn't it stir up the old people! They had never heard a word about it! My letter to them, posted at the same time with the proposal, had been delayed in London. The young lady went to Scotland, and was with them two weeks, and came away having made such an impression on them that they wrote me from home to say that 'though I searched the country for a couple years I could not have made a better choice.'

"Perhaps I am tiring you, but I want to let you know all about it and to assure you that you need not be the least shy of me or of my English wife. She is a good lassie, any quantity better than me, and just as handy as a Scotch lass would have been. It was great fun for her to read your tirade about English wives and your warning about her. She is a jolly kind of body, and does not take offense, but I guess if she comes across you she will wake you up a bit."

- Richard Lovett, editor and arranger. *James Gilmour of Mongolia; His Diaries, Letters and Reports.* Chicago: Student Missionary Campaign Library, [1892].

Gilpin, Bernard (1517-1583). A Fortuitous Break; his Boldness.

Bernard Gilpin was an English priest who sided with the Reformation, and a theologian of great grace, who became known as "the Apostle of the North" because of his work around Houghton, England.

Broken leg. WHEN BERNARD GILPIN answered his summons to be tried by Roman Catholic authorities in London for his Protestant beliefs, he provided himself with a long garment in which to burn at the stake, fully expecting to suffer martyrdom. On the way, he fell and broke his leg, which forced a temporary halt to the journey.

Now Gilpin had often said that nothing happens to the people of God but what is intended for their good. The person who had custody of him used the occasion to remind him of his saying and to ask him whether his broken leg was intended for good.

"I make no question but it is," replied Gilpin. He was right. Before he could travel again, Queen Mary died. With Protestant Elizabeth ascending the throne, there was no more talk of trying him, and he returned to Houghton where crowds gathered to congratulate him and rejoice at his deliverance.

- Adapted from several sources, including "Gilpin, Bernard." *Dictionary of National Biography*. Edited by Leslie Stephen and Sidney Lee. London: Oxford University Press, 1921-1996; William Gilpin's *Life of Bernard Gilpin*. London: John and James Rivington, 1753; and Walter Baxendale's *Dictionary of Anecdote, Incident, Illustrative Fact*. New York: Thomas Whittaker, 1889.

Boldness before his bishop. ONCE GILPIN HAD PREPARED for a preaching tour through the spiritually neglected areas of North England. Before he left, he received a message from Dr. Barns, bishop of Durham, appointing him to preach a sermon the following Sunday. He explained his prior engagement and excused himself. Hearing no more about it, he assumed his excuse was accepted and started off. On his return, he found himself suspended from his pulpit.

Dr. Barns commanded him to appear before him and a gathering of unfriendly clergymen, and when he arrived, ordered him to preach on the spot. Gilpin reminded them of his suspension, and pointed out that he was unprepared. He was ordered to preach anyhow and took as his theme the awful responsibility of a Christian bishop. He blasted the corruption of the clergy, and warned Bishop Barns that he was guilty if he allowed clergy crimes to continue with his knowledge. At the judgment, he, Bernard Gilpin, would himself testify against his bishop.

Gilpin's friends scolded him for these daring words, but he said he only hoped the sermon would attain its purpose. However, he visited his bishop to pay his respects. Dr. Barns, far from expressing anger, said Gilpin was more worthy of being bishop than himself. The bishop promised he would allow none of Gilpin's clergyman-enemies to trouble him any more.

- Among sources for this anecdote are William Gilpin's *Life of Bernard Gilpin*. London: John and James Rivington, 1753; and C. Matthew MacMahon's *Memoirs of the Puritans,* an online collection.

Girard, Catalan (died ca. 1537). Object Lesson Amid Flames.

The Waldenses were a Christian sect who originated in France in the eleventh century. They translated the scripture into their own language and rejected many trappings of the medieval church, including the mass, which they considered unbiblical. Not content to hold truth themselves, they sent peddlers as missionaries. Pope Innocent III ordered the Waldenses exterminated, which brought upon them suffering which historians have found too terrible to report in detail. But the brave Waldenses employed the mountains as fortresses and defended their faith and the virtue of their wives and daughters. Here is the last act of one brave martyr.

ONE OF THE MARTYRS, Catalan Girard, quaintly taught the spectators a parable, standing at the stake. From amid the flames he asked for two stones, which were instantly brought him. The crowd looked on in silence, curious to know what he meant to do with them. Rubbing them against each other, he said, "You think to extinguish our poor churches by your persecutions. You can no more do so than I with my feeble hands can crush these stones."

- J.A. Wylie. *History of the Waldenses.* Washington, D. C. : Review and Herald Publishing Association, [1880].

Godfrey of Bouillon (ca. 1060-1100). Rejects Royal Emblems.

Godfrey responded with alacrity to Pope Urban's call for the First Crusade. Ignorant and superstitious, but shrewd and devout, he proved (according to the historian Edward Gibbon) to be the most capable and honorable of the Latin leaders. He and his knights were first over the wall of Jerusalem.

EIGHT DAYS AFTER the conquerors of Jerusalem presented themselves before the Shrine of the Holy Sepulcher in the first crusade, the chiefs of the crusaders met to select a king to govern Palestine for them. As Gibbon tells it, "...the unanimous voice of the army proclaimed Godfrey of Bouillion the first and most worthy of the champions of Christendom. His magnanimity accepted a trust as full of danger as of glory; but in a city where his Savior had been crowned with thorns, the devout pilgrim rejected the name and ensigns of royalty; and the founder of the kingdom of Jerusalem contented himself with the modest title of Defender and Baron of the Holy Sepulcher."

- See chapter 58 in Edward Gibbon's *The Decline and Fall of the Roman Empire.*

Goodwin, Thomas (1600-1679). Dying Words.

Thomas Goodwin was a notable Congregational preacher and author in seventeenth-century England, who suffered considerable persecution during his life.

"Ah, is this dying? How I have dreaded as an enemy this smiling friend."

- This quotation appears in many internet sources and in Herbert Lockyer's *Last Words of Saints and Sinners*. Grand Rapids: Kregel, 1975.

Gregory the Great (ca. 540-604). As Anecdotalist; Despising Wealth.

Gregory the Great was pope at a time when Roman government had collapsed. Italy turned to the church for leadership and this able man provided it. He also wrote much instructional material filled with superstition and improbable miracles. Highly influential, this nonsense helped set the credulous tone of the middle ages. Here is an anecdote, said to be one of the best from his Dialogues *followed by an assessment of Gregory's charity and his opinion of wealth.*

A moral tale from Gregory. THE GARDENER OF A MONASTERY, finding that a thief stole his vegetables, set a snake to watch the place in the hedge where the thief was accustomed to break in, saying, "In the name of Jesus I bid you keep this passage and suffer no thief to enter." The snake stretched itself obediently across the way, and the monk then returned to his cell. Presently, when the brethren were all taking their midday siesta, the thief came; but just as he was climbing in, he caught sight of the snake. In his fear he fell back, and his shoe catching in a stake, he was hung up head downwards, without any means of extricating himself from his position. The snake meanwhile continued to watch him until the gardener returned and dismissed it from duty.

Gregory's unconcern for wealth. A CERTAIN HERMIT of great virtue, who possessed nothing in the world but a cat, which he often caressed and fondled in his bosom, prayed God to show him the reward he would get hereafter for giving up so entirely the riches of this world. It was revealed to him in the night that he should share a heavenly mansion with Gregory, the Roman Pope. At this the holy man was grieved, thinking that his voluntary poverty would be poorly rewarded if he obtained nothing more than one who lived amid such abundance and worldly wealth.

Day and night, with sighs and groans, he compared his own destitution with Gregory's riches, until at last God said to him in a dream, "It is not the possession of riches, but the lust for them that makes a rich man; why then do you dare to compare your poverty with the riches of Gregory? You, in loving your cat, and stroking it daily and giving it to no one, are more enamored of wealth than he, who does not love his great riches, but dispenses them to all men liberally." The hermit thanked God for His rebuke, and afterwards prayed earnestly that he might be counted worthy to share a mansion with the world-despising pope.

- From Dudden F. Homes' *Gregory the Great; His place in history and thought*. London, New York and Bombay. Longmans, Green and co., 1905.

Grenfell, Wilfred (1865-1940). A Proposal Like None Other.

The Englishman Wilfred Grenfell was famous for his adventures as a North Sea doctor and then as a missionary doctor in Labrador. In 1909, he traveled on the Mauretania with his elderly mother, who was traveling to see him presented with honorary degrees at Harvard University and Williams College.

ABOARD THE *MAURETANIA*, Grenfell was attracted by a regal-looking but somewhat frivolous young lady. He did not know her name (Anne Elizabeth McClanahan) but, as she was traveling with the Chicago banker W. R. Stirling, he assumed she was the banker's daughter and sat down in a deck chair beside her one day.

Addressing her by the Stirling name, he chided her gently for her useless life as a young society lady. Naturally, she was indignant. "You don't even know my name," she retorted, "and talk to me like this!"

Grenfell wrote later, "Had I not been a bit of a seaman and often compelled on the spur of the moment to act first and think afterwards, what the consequences might have been I cannot say. Fortunately I remembered that it was not the matter at issue, and explained, without admitting the impeachment, that the only question that interested me in the least was what I hoped [her name] might become."

They were married that year in Chicago and she returned to work with him in Labrador.

- J. Lennox Kerr,. *Wilfred Grenfell, His Life and Work*. New York: Dodd, Mead and Co., 1959; Grenfell, Wilfrid. A Labrador Doctor; the autobiography of Wilfred Thomason Grenfell. Boston: Houghton Mifflin, 1919.

Grindal, Edmund (1519-1583). Preserved by His Love of Reading.

Few men defied Elizabeth I of England and lived to tell of it. Edmund Grindal, the gentle but courageous Archbishop of Canterbury was one. Ordered to put a stop to "prophesying," a popular form of preaching not unlike a public debate, Grindal refused in a lengthy, well-reasoned letter that infuriated Elizabeth by politely telling her to mind the affairs of state and allow bishops to mind the affairs of the church. Although she did not execute him, Elizabeth placed him under house arrest for the remainder of his life. There was a touch of the miraculous in Grindal's life, both then and as a youth.

OF EDMUND GRINDAL'S family and early history little is known. One remarkable incident from his boyhood is on record, however, and it shows his diligence in learning. Books were the companion of his walks, and on one occasion a book preserved his life. While he was walking in the fields, an arrow plunged against his chest, and if a book had not intercepted it, would probably have killed him.

- Adapted from William Nicholson's *The Remains of Edmund Grindal; successively bishop of London and archbishop of York and Canterbury*. Cambridge University Press, 1843.

Ham, Mordecai (1877-1961). Sinner in a Cornfield.

Mordecai Ham was a southern evangelist who led thousands to Christ, including Billy Graham. His luster was dimmed by his anti-Semitism, but he was a bold soul-winner.

HAM CONTINUALLY CHALLENGED sin and sinners. In one notable instance, he confronted an infidel who was hiding in a cornfield to avoid him.

"What are you going to do?" asked this opponent of the Gospel.

"Ask God to kill you," replied Ham. The infidel protested. Ham said that since the man claimed to believe there was no God, such a prayer shouldn't bother him in the least. Nonetheless the unbeliever begged Ham not to pray for his death, so Ham agreed to pray for his salvation instead. The man was converted on the spot.

- Retold from James A. Borland's "Mordecai Ham, a Thorn in the Devil's Side." *Fundamentalist Journal* 3 (February, 1984) 44-46.

Handel, George Frederick (1685-1759). A Late Change of Character; Playing the People Out.

Handel, born in Germany, transplanted to England, where he became one of the most notable composers of his day. His most famous and beloved work is the oratorio Messiah *which is usually sung at Christmas time.*

Handel in heaven? HANDEL COMPOSED TUNES expressly for Charles Wesley's hymns. He set music to those beginning "Sinners obey the Gospel word," "O love divine, how sweet thou art!" and "Rejoice, the Lord is King." The musical manuscripts, in Handel's own handwriting, are preserved at the Cambridge  University. Handel was so profane, and had a temper so ungovernable, that he would swear in seven different languages; and yet Charles Wesley, in a beautiful elegy on the death of Dr. Boyce, places him in heaven among the worshipers before the throne of God:

> "...Where Handel strikes the golden strings,
> And plausive angels strike their wings."

Charles Wesley did not believe that Handel's transcendent musical genius would save him, but rather an alteration in character. Handel lost his property, and toward the close of life became blind. A wonderful change passed over him. He regularly attended divine worship, and exhibited a spirit of deep devotion. Charles Wesley therefore had reason for representing the great composer of The Messiah striking his golden harp with angels and archangels before the throne of God.

- Adapted from J. B. Wakelet's *Anecdotes of the Wesleys; Illustrative of Their Character and Personal History.* New York: Carlton & Lanahan; Cincinnati: Hitchcock & Walden, 1869.

Playing the congregation out. ONE SUNDAY, having attended divine worship at a country church, Handel asked the organist to permit him to play the people out; to which, with a politeness characteristic of the profession, the organist consented. Handel accordingly sat down to the organ, and began to play in such a masterly manner, as instantly to attract the attention of the whole congregation, who, instead of vacating their seats as usual, remained fixed in silent admiration. The organist began to be impatient; and at length addressing the performer, told him that he was convinced that he could not play the people out, and advised him to relinquish the attempt; which being done, they were played out in the usual manner.

- *The Book of Three Hundred Anecdotes Historical, Literary, and Humorous—A New Selection.* London and New York: Burns & Oates, n.d.

Harris, Samuel (Eighteenth Century). Christ's Bail.

Samuel Harris, an evangelist in colonial Virginia, established at least 25 Baptist churches.

SHORTLY AFTER HE BEGAN TO PREACH, Samuel Harris was informed by one of his debtors that he did not intend paying him the debt he owed "unless he sued him." Harris left the man's presence meditating.

"What shall I do?" he wondered, for he badly needed the money. "Must I leave preaching and attend to a vexatious lawsuit? Perhaps a thousand souls will perish in the meantime."

He turned aside into a woods and sought guidance in prayer. Rising from his knees, he resolved to hold the man no longer a debtor, and at once wrote out a receipt in full, which he sent by a servant. Shortly after, the man met him and demanded what he meant. "I mean," said Harris, "Just what I wrote."

"But you know I never paid you," replied the debtor.

"True," Harris answered; "and I know you said that you never would unless I sued. But, sir, I sued you at the court of heaven, and Christ has entered bail for you; I have therefore given you a discharge."

"But I insist matters shall not be left so," replied the man.

"I am well satisfied," replied Harris. "Jesus will not fail me. I leave you to settle the account with Him another day. Farewell!"

This operated so effectually on the man's conscience that in a few days he came and paid the debt.

- Adapted from Walter Baxendale's *Dictionary of Anecdote, Incident, Illustrative Fact*. New York: Thomas Whittaker, 1889.

Harvie, Marion (died 1681). Truth on the Scaffold.

Marion Harvie had been a godless young Scotswoman until converted under Covenanter preaching. The Covenanters believed that Christ, not the King of England, was head of the church. At her trial she spoke staunchly for Christ and the Covenanter cause, for which she was sentenced to die. As her hanging approached, she stuck fast to her bold words.

"THEY SAY, I WOULD MURDER, but I declare, I am free of all matters of fact [that is, not guilty of any actual crime]; I could never take the life of a chicken, but my heart shrinked. But it is only for my judgment of things [opinions] that I am brought here. I leave my blood on the council, and the Duke of York." At this the soldiers interrupted her, and would not allow her to speak any: But she cried out, "I leave my blood on all ungodly and profane wretches."

The most of her discourse was of God's love to her, and the commendation of free grace; and she declared she had much of the Lord's presence with her in prison, and said, "I bless the Lord, the snare is broken, and we are escaped [from sin];" and when she came to the ladder-foot, she prayed. And going up the ladder, she said, "O my fair one, my lovely one, come away;" and sitting down upon the ladder, she said, "I am not come here for murder, for they have no matter of fact to charge me with, but only my judgment [opinions]. I am about twenty years of age; at fourteen or fifteen I was a hearer of these [the lifeless Christian leaders], I was a blasphemer and Sabbath-breaker, and a chapter of the Bible was a burden to me; but since I heard this persecuted Gospel [Covenanter preaching], I durst not [dared not] blaspheme, nor break the Sabbath, and the Bible became my delight." With this the major called to the hangman to cast her over, and the murderer presently choked her.

- *A Cloud of Witnesses for the Royal Prerogatives of Jesus Christ, or, the last speeches and testimonies of those who have suffered for the truth in Scotland since the year 1680.* Glasgow: J. Gilmour and Son, etc., 1769.

Hastings, Lady Selina (1707-1791). Ardor Rebuffed.

Selina Hastings lived an exemplary and dutiful life as a young woman and mother, but was tormented with uncertainty of her salvation until she put her trust in Christ. Then everyone noticed a difference in her and her works became effectual for spreading the Gospel.

SELINA WROTE TO EMINENT WOMEN in society and implored them to forsake their sins and turn their gaze upon Christ and heed the words of evangelists such as George Whitefield and John Wesley. The Duchess of Buckingham replied, "The doctrines of these preachers are most  repulsive and strongly tinctured with impertinence and disrespect toward their superiors, in perpetually endeavoring to level all ranks and do away with all distinctions. It is monstrous to be told that you have a heart as sinful as the common wretches that crawl upon the earth. This is highly offensive and insulting, and I cannot but wonder that your ladyship should relish any sentiments so much at variance with high rank and good breeding."

- Helen C. Knight. *Lady Huntington and Her Friends.* New York: American Tract Society, 1853.

Haydn, Franz Joseph (1732-1809). First London Performance of The Creation.

Haydn held Deist views and lived openly with another man's wife. However, in his old age, he composed the oratorio The Creation. *Of this he said, "Never was I so pious as when composing* The Creation. *I felt myself so penetrated with religious feeling that before I sat down to the pianoforte I prayed to God*

with earnestness that He would enable me to praise Him worthily." Of its first London performance the following amusing anecdote is told.

SALOMON NOW WROTE to the composer for a copy of the score, so that he might produce the oratorio in London. He was, however, beaten out by John Ashley, who was giving performances of oratorios in those days at Convent Garden Theatre, and who brought forward the new work on the 28th of March (1800).

The score arrived by a King's messenger from Vienna on Saturday, March 22, at nine o'clock in the evening. It was handed to Thomas Goodwin, the theater's copyist, who immediately set to work to have the parts copied out for 120 performers, a feat which involved a good deal of reworking. The performance took place on the following Friday evening, and when Mr. Harris, the proprietor of the theater, complimented all parties concerned on their promptitude, Goodwin, with ready wit, replied: "Sir, we have humbly emulated a great example; it is not the first time that the Creation has been completed in six days."

• Adapted from J. Cuthbert Hadden. *Haydn. The Master Musicians series*. London: J. M. Dent & Co.; New York: E. P. Dutton & Co., 1902.

Haynes, Lemuel (1754-1833). Devil Spawn.

Lemuel Haynes fought in the Revolutionary War then became a pastor, one of the first African-Americans to preach to Caucasian congregations.

SHORTLY AFTER HAYNES PUBLISHED A SERMON on the text, "Ye shall not surely die," two reckless young men plotted to test his wit. One said, "Father Haynes, have you heard the good news?"

"No," said Haynes. "What is it?"

"It is great news, indeed," said the other. "And, if true, your business is done."

"What is it?" inquired the preacher again.

"Why," responded the first, "the devil is dead."

Lifting both of his hands and placing them on the heads of the messengers of this "intelligence," Haynes said with deep commiseration, "Oh you poor, fatherless children! What will become of you?"

- Adapted from Walter Baxendale's *Dictionary of Anecdote, Incident, Illustrative Fact*. New York: Thomas Whittaker, 1889.

Hennuyer, Jean, Bishop of Lisieux (died 1578). Rejects St. Bartholomew Day Massacre.

In the St. Bartholomew's Day Massacre, Catholics first assassinated the Protestant leader Coligny and then killed thousands of unoffending Huguenots in Paris and throughout the rest of France. It is considered the most vicious of the century's religious massacres.

THE MASSACRE OF ST. BARTHOLOMEW was not confined to Paris; orders were sent to the most distant provinces to commence the work of destruction. When the governor of the province brought the order to Hennuyer, Bishop of Lisieux, he opposed it with all his power, and caused a formal act of his opposition to be entered on the registers of the province. Charles IX, when remorse had taken the place of cruelty, was so far from disapproving of what this excellent prelate had done, that he gave him the greatest praise for his humanity; and Protestants flocked in numbers to adjure their religion at the feet of this good and kind shepherd, whose gentleness affected them more than either the commands of the sovereign, or the violence of the soldiery.

- *The Book of Three Hundred Anecdotes Historical, Literary, and Humorous—A New Selection.* London and New York: Burns & Oates, n.d.

Henry, Philip (1631-1696). A Mantle of Love.

Philip Henry was a Presbyterian minister, the father of Matthew Henry—who authored the well-known Bible Commentary that bears his name

PHILIP HENRY USED TO REMIND those who spoke evil of people behind their backs of that law, "You shall not curse the deaf." Those who are absent are deaf; they cannot defend themselves; therefore say no ill of them. A friend of his, inquiring of him concerning a matter which tended to reflect upon some people, he began to give him an account of the story, but immediately broke off, and checked himself with these words, "But our rule is to speak evil of no man," and would proceed no further in the story. The week before he died, someone requested the loan of a certain book from him. "Truly," said he, "I would lend it to you, but that it takes in the faults of some which should rather be covered with a mantle of love."

- Walter Baxendale's *Dictionary of Anecdote, Incident, Illustrative Fact.* New York: Thomas Whittaker, 1889.

Henry VIII (1491-1547). The Subversive Word.

Henry VIII is one of England's best-known monarchs, infamous for executing several of his own wives.

IT IS POSSIBLE TO DO THE RIGHT THING for the wrong reason, in which case the "good deed" is not a praiseworthy action. A case in point is found in the actions of King Henry VIII.

During the Reformation, he opposed for many years allowing his own people to have Bibles. At the same time, he had Bibles smuggled into Scotland. Scotland, you will recall, was not yet united with England. In all this, Henry was not inconsistent. He opposed Bibles for England because he felt they made it harder to unify and govern people. He sent Bibles to Scotland for the same reason: he wished to subvert the rival government.

- This fact is mentioned in Whitley's biography of John Knox.

Herbert, George (1593-1633). Common vs. Midnight Music.

At one point, George Herbert considered seeking high political office, but instead fixed his ambition on being the best churchman he could. He was devoted to his parishioners at Bemerton, and they loved him, calling him

"Holy Mr. Herbert." He is famed for his poems, the greatest of which have Christian themes.

HIS CHIEF RECREATION was music, in which heavenly art he was a most excellent master, and composed many divine hymns and anthems, which he set to music and sang to his lute or viol: and though he preferred to be in the quiet of his home rather than out and about, yet his love for music was such, that almost every week he went twice, on set days, to the Cathedral Church in Salisbury; and on his return would say his time spent in prayer, and cathedral-music, elevated his soul, and was his heaven upon earth. Before his return to Bemerton, he would usually sing and play at a private music gathering; and, to justify this practice, he would often say, "Religion does not banish mirth, but only moderates and sets rules to it."

On one walk to Salisbury to make music, he saw a poor man with a poorer horse, which was fallen under its load. Both were in distress, and needed immediate help. George Herbert took off his canonical coat, and helped the poor man to unload, and afterward to reload, his horse. The poor man blessed him for it, and he blessed the poor man; and was so like the good Samaritan, that he gave him money to refresh both himself and his horse; and told him, If he loved himself he should be merciful to his beast.

Having left the poor man and arrived to the home of his musical friends at Salisbury, they were astonished that he, who usually was so trim and clean, entered the room so dirty and untidy: but he explained what had happened. Then one of his friends told him he had lowered himself by stooping to such a dirty task. Herbert answered that the thought of what he had done would prove music to him at midnight; and that if he had not acted as he had, his conscience would have troubled him every time he passed that place; "for if I be bound to pray for everyone who is in distress, I am sure that I am bound, so far as it is in my power, to practice what I pray for. And though I do not wish for a similar occasion every day, yet let me tell you, I would not willingly pass one day of my life without comforting a sad soul, or showing mercy; and I praise God for this occasion. And now let us tune our instruments."

- Adapted from Sir Izaac Walton's *Lives of John Donne, Henry Wotton, Rich'd Hooker, George Herbert, &C,* Volume Two. John Major's Edition, 1925.

Hill, Rowland (1744-1833). Witticisms.

Rowland Hill was a witty Church of England pastor who pastored the rough and poor and preached in the fields like George Whitefield. He was often censured by brethren who thought him eccentric, but the common folk loved to hear him. Below are some of his famous sallies.

Anonymous letter. MR. HAYWARD RECALLS to us, in one of his essays, Rowland Hill's reply when, on one occasion, he read from his pulpit an anonymous letter reproaching him with driving to chapel in his carriage, and reminding him that this was not our blessed Lord's mode of traveling. He said, "I must admit that it is not. But if the writer of this letter will come here next Sunday, bridled and saddled, I shall have the pleasure of following our blessed Lord's example in that as in all other matters within my power."

- W. Davenport Adams. *Modern Anecdotes; a treasury of wise and witty sayings of the last hundred years.* London, Hamilton, Adams, 1886.

A cane substitute. ROWLAND HILL once witnessed the ordination of a minister in Scotland, and one of the elders of the Presbytery, not being able to reach his hand far enough to impose it on the head of the candidate, used the end of his cane for the purpose. "This," said Mr. Hill, "did equally well; it was timber to timber."

- W. Davenport Adams. *Modern Anecdotes; a treasury of wise and witty sayings of the last hundred years.* London, Hamilton, Adams, 1886.

His enthusiasm reproached. ROWLAND HILL was sometimes completely carried away by the impetuous rush of his feelings. On one such occasion, while preaching at Wotton, he exclaimed, "Because I am in earnest, men call me an enthusiast. But I am not; mine are the words of truth and soberness. When I first came into this part of the country I was working on yonder hill. I saw a gravel pit fall in and bury three human beings alive. I lifted up my voice for help so loud that I was heard in the town below, at the distance of a mile. Help came and rescued the poor sufferers. No one called me an enthusiast then. And when I see eternal destruction ready to fall upon poor sinners, and I call aloud to them to escape, shall I be called an enthusiast now?"

- Adapted from Walter Baxendale's *Dictionary of Anecdote, Incident, Illustrative Fact.* New York: Thomas Whittaker, 1889.

Hooker, Richard (1554-1600). His Less than Ideal Marriage; Prey to Blackmail.

Richard Hooker was an English theologian and priest, whose writings called for tolerance and inclusiveness and helped shape Anglican thought.

His marriage. IN FINDING A WIFE, John Hooker trusted far more to another than most men would. A Mrs. Churchman, having nursed him through an illness, convinced him he needed a wife to care for him. He said he would marry whomever she chose. Mrs. Churchman planted one of her own ill-favored daughters on him, who proved less of a comfort than an affliction to him.

His pupil George Cranmer, after spending a night with him, commiserated him as they parted the next day. "Good tutor, I am sorry your lot is fallen in no better ground, as to your parsonage; and more sorry that your wife proves not a more comfortable companion, after you have wearied yourself in your restless studies."

To this Hooker replied, "My dear George, if saints have usually a double share in the miseries of this life, I, who am not one, ought not to repine at what my wise Creator has appointed for me: but labor—as indeed I do daily—to submit my will to his will, and possess my soul in patience and peace."

Blackmail. HOOKER HARDLY KNEW how to handle the hurly-burly world. When a depraved woman entered his room, and demanded money, threatening to accuse him of sexual advances if he did not pay up, he meekly met her demands. She repeated her demand on other occasions. Once when she appeared, two of Hooker's pupils were present. They were surprised that he allowed a person of her character into his house and questioned him about it, upon which he explained her demands and threats.

The two young men hid themselves in the room the next time the woman came, listened to her threats, verified the facts, and popped out of their hiding place. The woman, along with those who put her up to the con job, were apprehended and punished.

• Both anecdotes are adapted from Sir Izaak Walton's *Lives*.

Howie, John (1735-1793). Do Weird Phenomena Betoken Disaster?

> *Howie was a Scot chronicler and biographer, who collected information about the Covenanters and issued a collection of short biographies under the title* Biographia Scoticana, or Scot Worthies. *He was also interested in weird phenomena. Today people lose themselves in the mysteries of crop circles and UFOs. In earlier eras, they read terrors into comets and eclipses, or reported phantom armies, dragons, and strange shapes and lights in the sky. Here is an example of the last with its "interpretation."*

A.D. 1626, JUNE 15th, between eight and nine in the morning, a strange phenomenon happened in Scotland: The sun shining bright, there appeared to the view of many, as it were, three suns one by east; another by fourth-east, with the true sun in appearance near it. From the fourthmost proceeded a luminary in form of a horn, that pointed north west, and carried with it, as it were, a gray rainbow, but clearer than the sky. This was thought by some to presage some future calamity; an apprehension in which they were not mistaken: for in Germany, the sword destroyed vast numbers of protestants; in France, the orb of the Gospel was almost extinguished; at home, King Charles pointed the horn of his resentment against the Scots Presbyterians who would not comply with prelacy and the five articles of Perth, which he pressed upon them with rigor. Archbishop Laud being now advanced to the helm of affairs, the mock suns of Popery and Arminianism made their way into the nations in a remarkable manner; in opposing which, several eminent lights of the church were reduced to a series of hardships.

- Adapted from John Howie's *An Alarm unto a Secure Generation, or a short historical relation of some of the most strange and remarkable appearances of comets, fiery meteors, bloody signs...etc.* Glasgow: John Bryce, 1780.

Hunt, John (1812-1848). Cannibals Pray for Dying Missionary.

After many trials and through much opposition from the islanders, John Hunt and his wife Hannah won the cannibals of Fiji to Christ. Weakened by his efforts, Hunt became ill, dying full of joy and glory at the young age of 36. This anecdote shows how the Fijians, transformed from their savage ways, responded to his illness.

THE PEOPLE, WITH SAD FACES, flocked that Saturday evening to the chapel, and bowed themselves before God. The voice of one after another was uplifted on behalf of their missionary. Elijah Verani cried aloud: "O Lord! we know we are very bad, but spare your servant. If one must die, take me! Take ten of us! But spare your servant to preach Christ to the people!"

- Adapted from George Stringer Rowe's *A Missionary among Cannibals: The Life of John Hunt...* New York: Sunday School Union, 1859.

Hyde, John (1865-1912). A Splitting Headache.

John "Praying" Hyde was a Spirit-filled missionary to India.

ONE DAY "Praying Hyde" woke with a headache so excruciating he could hardly bear it. Since it was his practice to thank God for everything, he thanked him aloud for this. At first he did not see how he could even pray, but decided he must not allow a headache to stand between him and souls. He asked helpers to place him under the shade of a tree. A number of women who had resisted becoming Christians came over to offer him sympathy. He seized the opportunity to speak to them of Christ. As a consequence, several of them were converted and decided to be baptized. "I now see the reason for the severe headache this morning," he said. "Without it I would not have been enabled to win these women."

- Retold from Basil Miller's *Praying Hyde*. Grand Rapids: Zondervan, 1943.

Inspector of Forests (Nineteenth Century). Inspector Rejoiced at Being Chained with Desperate Convicts.

When faith captures a man, unlikely results follow.

THE MEETINGS FOR PRAYER at this time in St. Petersburg were like those of the Primitive Church, and remarkable and instantaneous were the answers. A woman possessed and blaspheming became infuriated when brought among the praying band; but the intercessors continued until midnight. At last the evil spirit was cast out and she fell senseless to the ground. She became an earnest Christian, and her husband, a drunkard and a skeptic, seeing the miracle performed on his wife, came to the meeting, was delivered from drink and eventually became Inspector of Colonel Paschkoff's forest near Moscow.

Here he discovered great dishonesty, and the guilty parties, to revenge themselves, accused him to the police of blaspheming icons, which was a great crime in Russia. Though innocent, he was sentenced to exile in Siberia for life. Chained to a gang of desperate characters to march a thousand miles on foot in cold that was 20° to 40° below zero, all hope of human help was abandoned.

Colonel Paschkoff hurried to Moscow to console him, but found him radiant with joy, saying, "How good the Lord is; I have been praying to work among prisoners and this is how my prayer is answered." Colonel Paschkoff had just time to slip a testament into his hand before he was marched off. A year later, in 1878, at one of the meetings of the McCall Mission in Paris, a gentleman asked leave to speak. He was a Jew by birth and had been a skeptic but when traveling in Russia some months previously, he had come across a batch of prisoners, one of whom attracted him by his happy face. He heard him say, "It is all joy," and, astonished, asked him his meaning. The prisoner then spoke of the love of God which filled his soul. "How did he know about this love?" asked the visitor, and the prisoner showed him the testament. The Jew begged to have it. It was the only book the prisoner possessed, but yielding to his entreaties, he relinquished it. "Now," said the Jew, "I, too, know that Jesus is the Messiah and the Savior."

- Adapted from Mrs. Edward Trotter's *Lord Radstock; an Interpretation and a Record.* London: Hodder & Stoughton, ca. 1914.

Jaffray, Robert (1873-1945). Boldness with Bandits.

Although plagued with a bad heart, Robert A. Jaffray abandoned a fortune and a secure career in his father's news empire, to become a missionary to the Far East. He had ability, vision, faith, and—as this anecdote shows—courage.

WHILE TRAVELING UP THE FU River with fellow missionaries, Robert Jaffray was captured by bandits. They stole everything they could strip off the boat and off the missionaries and demanded "toll." Jaffrey responded by telling their leader he and his companions were bearers of the Gospel, who were used to receiving gifts to preach the word of God. He asked the bandits to release them and give them something to help them on their way. The bandits appreciated his courage, but held the missionaries captive for ransom.

The trip was arduous, but so great was the respect Jaffray gained in the eyes of the robbers that they treated the missionaries with consideration. Eventually the bandits brought their captives to smoke-filled caves.

Again and again Jaffray spoke to the men and women of Christ. He could intimidate them or throw them into gales of laughter. Although the bandits were brutal and openly engaged in animal-like acts of lust, they responded with tears when he told them of Christ's forgiveness.

Eventually they sent Jaffray and another missionary to raise a ransom, at which he was successful. At the start of the ordeal, Jaffray had feared for his heart, but his heavy exertion during the forced marches strengthened him, and his health improved from that point on.

- Retold from A. W. Tozer's *Let My People Go; the Life of Robert A. Jaffray.* Camp Hill, Pennsylvania: Christian Publications, 1990.

Jerome (ca. 347-420). The Difference Friendship Makes.

Jerome was a scholar, the translator of the Bible into Latin.

WHILE RUFINUS was St. Jerome's friend, the Bible scholar praised him as the most learned man of his age; but when the Rufinus translated the works of Origen (which Jerome despised), he called him one of the most ignorant!

- Adapted from Isaac D'Israeli's *Curiosities of Literature*. London: Frederick and Warne, 1881.

Jogues, Isaac (1607-1646). Duty Outweighs Self-Preservation.

A scholarly, well-educated young Frenchman, Isaac Jogues traded a life of books for one of missionary heroism in the wilds of North America. He was the first missionary to reach Michigan and discovered what is now known as Lake George.

IN THE EARLY MORNING of the second of August, 1642, twelve Huron canoes were moving slowly along the northern shore of the expansion of the St. Lawrence known as the Lake of St. Peter. On board were about forty persons, including four Frenchmen, one of them being the Jesuit, Isaac Jogues...who sat in one of the leading canoes. ...

The twelve canoes had reached the western end of the Lake of St. Peter, where it is filled with innumerable islands, The forest was close on their right, they kept near the shore to avoid the current, and the shallow water before them was covered with a dense growth of tall bulrushes. Suddenly the silence was frightfully broken. A war-whoop rose from among the rushes, mingled with reports of guns and the whistling of bullets; and several Iroquois canoes, filled with warriors, pushed out from concealment, and bore down upon Jogues and his companions. The Hurons in the rear were seized with a shameful panic. They leaped ashore; left canoes, baggage and weapons; and fled into the woods. The

French and the Christian Hurons fought for a time; but when they saw another fleet of canoes approaching from the opposite shores or islands, they lost heart, and those escaped who could. Goupil [a young priest] was seized amid triumphant yells, as were also several of the Huron converts. Jogues sprang into the bulrushes and might have escaped; but when he saw Goupil and the neophytes in the clutches of the Iroquois, he had no heart to abandon them, but came out from his hiding-place, and gave himself up to the astonished victors. A few of them had remained to guard the prisoners; the rest were chasing the fugitives. Jogues began to baptize those converts who needed baptism.

The Iroquois then ripped out his fingernails and gnawed his fingers to the bone. With their captives they set out on a triumphant eight day march. "The pain and fever of their wounds, and the clouds of mosquitoes, which they could not drive off, left the prisoners no peace by day nor sleep by night." They met up with other Iroquois warriors. They were forced to run the gauntlet. At night when they longed to sleep, young warriors lacerated their wounds and plucked their beards. At village after village they were again forced to run the gauntlet and were tortured over and over. At night they were tied down between stakes and children dropped burning coals on their bodies. One day Jogues was hung by his arms between poles.

While they were in this town, four fresh Huron prisoners, just taken, were brought in, and placed on the scaffold with the rest. Jogues, in the midst of his pain and exhaustion, took the opportunity to convert them. An ear of green corn was thrown to him for food, and he discovered a few rain-drops clinging to the husks. With these he baptized two of the Hurons. The remaining two he baptized soon afterward from a brook which the prisoners crossed on their way to another town.

Jogues and Goupil expected to be burned to death like several of the Hurons. Nonetheless, Jogues continued to baptize dying children. Goupil was tomahawked for making the sign of the cross on a child.

Jogues had shown no disposition to escape, and great liberty was therefore allowed him. He went from town to town, giving absolution to the Christian captives, and converting and baptizing the heathen. On one occasion he baptized a woman who was in the midst of the fire, under pretense of lifting a cup of water to her parched lips. There was no lack of objects for his zeal. A single war party returned from the Huron country with nearly a hundred prisoners, who were distributed among the Iroquois towns, and the greater part burned. Of the children of the Mohawks and their neighbors, he had baptized before August, about seventy; insomuch that he began to regard his captivity as a Providential interposition for the saving of souls...

When given an opportunity to escape, Jogues wrestled all night whether he should or not, fearing that escape would be forsaking his duty. He did finally escape, and the Dutch paid ransom for him when the Indians threatened retaliation. He returned to France for a year, and then came back to work among the Indians of Canada where he was killed by the Mohawks. His killer became a Christian convert.

- Adapted from Francis Parkman's *The Jesuits in North America in the Seventeenth Century*. Boston: Little, Brown, and co. 1886.

Jones, E. Stanley (1884-1973). Not God's Lawyer.

Well-known as a Methodist missionary to India, and to the world at large, Eli Stanley Jones urged freeing Christianity from western cultural forms and allowing Indians to develop an indigenous interpretation of the Gospel message. Early in his ministry he learned to be God's witness rather than His advocate.

THIS LESSON OF BEING A WITNESS was burned into my very being by a tragic beginning of my Christian ministry. When I was called to the ministry I had a vague notion that I was to be God's lawyer—I was to argue his case for him and put it up brilliantly. When I told my pastor of my call he surprised and thoroughly frightened me by asking me to preach my first sermon on a certain Sunday night. I prepared very thoroughly, for I was anxious to make a good impression and argue His case acceptably. There was a large crowd there full of expectancy, for they wished the young man well.

I began on rather a high key. I had not gone a half dozen sentences when I used a word I had never used before (nor have I used it since!) - "indifferentism." I saw a college girl in the audience put down her head and smile. It so upset me that when I came back to the thread of my discourse, it was gone— absolutely. I do not know how long I stood there rubbing my hands, hoping that something would come back. It seemed like forever. Finally I blurted out, "Friends, I am very sorry, but I have forgotten my sermon!"

I started down the steps leading from the pulpit in shame and confusion. This was the beginning of my ministry, I thought— a tragic failure. As I was about to leave the pulpit a Voice seemed to say to me, "Haven't I done anything for you?"

"Yes," I replied, "You have done everything for me."

"Well," said the Voice, "couldn't you tell them that?"

"Yes, I suppose I could," I eagerly replied. So instead of going to my seat I came around in front of the pulpit below (I felt very lowly by this time and was persuaded I did not belong up there!) and said: "Friends, I see I cannot preach, but I love Jesus Christ. You know what my life was in this community—that of a wild, reckless young man—and you know what it now is. You know he has made life new for me, and though I cannot preach I am determined to love and serve him."

At the close a lad came up and said, "Stanley, I wish I could find what you have found." He did find it then and there. He is a member of that church now—a fine Christian man. No one congratulated me on that sermon that night, but after the sting of it had passed away, I have been congratulating myself ever since. The Lord let me down with a terrible thump, but I got the lesson never to be forgotten: In my ministry I was to be, not God's lawyer, but his witness. That would mean that there would have to be living communion with Christ so that there would always be something to pass on. Since that day I have tried to witness before high and low what Christ has been to an unworthy life.

- E. Stanley Jones. *The Christ of the Indian Road.* New York: Abingdon Press, 1925, p. 141ff.

Jones, Sam P. (1848-1906). How He Left His Meanness Behind.

Samuel Porter Jones was an alcoholic. His efforts to reform himself failed. Change began in him through a promise he made to his dying father—a promise he kept. Through the assistance of the Holy Spirit, he found new life in Christ and became a notable and witty evangelist in the South. In a typical instance, one committee called him to their town to preach to sinners. They were offended when he preached to them instead. Upon their complaining to him, Jones replied, "Never mind, I will get to the sinners. I never scald hogs until the water is hot." His brand of humor is said to have influenced Will Rogers.

HIS FATHER WAS SICK for several weeks, and it was the custom of the ministers to call and have prayers with him. Mr. Jones would attend these prayer services around his father's bedside. As the end came nearer, Captain Jones would tell of the presence of the Lord, and speak in such a way as to make every one feel that God truly was present. He would take his friends by the hand and in a cool, calm, delightful way say, "This little home that God has given me for my wife and children is filled with the glory of the Lord. I am physically very weak, but spiritually I am strong. When every other prop fails me, then Jesus Christ stands firm."

Just before the end came, he turned to each member of his family and spoke a parting word. Sam was standing at the foot of the bed, looking down into his father's face. When his father came to him for a moment he was speechless, while looking into his son's face. Finally he said, "My poor, wicked, wayward, reckless boy. You have broken the heart of your sweet wife and brought me down in sorrow to my grave; promise me, my boy, to meet me in heaven." Convulsed with emotion from head to foot, Sam stepped around to the side of the bed and took his father's bony hand in his and said: "Father, I'll make you the promise, I'll quit! I'll quit! I'll quit!" He said it in such a way that his dying father had every assurance that he meant it. A change was seen in his father's countenance, and the pledge from his boy, he believed, meant the reformation of his life.

Then and there Jones burned his bridges behind him, and walked away from the dying couch determined to live for the right. In after years, including some of his last utterances in Oklahoma City, Jones said, "Thank God, I can say every willful step of my life since that moment has been towards the redemption of that promise."

When Jones turned from the bedside of his dying father he was groping in darkness and in search of Jesus Christ the Savior of sinners. While the promise he made his father was a step toward salvation, and helped to bring about a speedy reformation, he was not entirely assured of his acceptance with God. After his father's death he went down to the home of his grandfather, Rev. Samuel G. Jones, on Saturday, and spent Sunday there. That morning his grandfather preached at Moore's Chapel. Jones was under deep conviction, and at the close of the sermon walked forward and gave his grandfather his hand, asking for the prayers of God's people.

His conviction became deeper each day, and he saw his sins as never before. While under the influence of the Holy Spirit, he had a glimpse of the cross. As Paul said, "The cross was a stumbling block to the Jew, and foolishness to the Greek," so it was with him until the light of the Holy Spirit flooded his soul.

• Adapted from *The Life and Sayings of Sam P. Jones* by his wife assisted by Rev. Walt Holcomb, a co-worker of Mr. Jones. Atlanta Georgia, Franklin-Turner Co, 1907.

Josquin des Prez (ca. 1450-1521). Music to Jog the King's Memory.

Josquin des Prez was a Franco-Flemish composer, the most significant writer of music between Dufay and Palestrina. He was an admirer of Savonarola.

JOSQUIN DES PREZ, the celebrated composer, was appointed master of the chapel to Louis XII of France, who promised him a benefice, but contrary to his usual custom, forgot him. Josquin, after suffering serious inconvenience from the shortness of his majesty's memory, ventured, by a singular expedient, publicly to remind him of his promise, without giving offence. Being commanded to compose a motet for the royal chapel, he chose the verse of the Psalm, "Oh, think of thy servant as concerning thy word," &c., which he set in so supplicating and exquisite a manner, that it was universally admired, particularly by the king, who was not only charmed with the music, but felt the force of the words so effectually, that he soon after granted his petition, by conferring on him the promised appointment. Upon receiving it, Josquin reportedly wrote a motet on the text Benefecisti servo tuo, Domine ("Lord, thou hast dealt graciously with thy servant") to show his gratitude to the king.

- *The Book of Three Hundred Anecdotes Historical, Literary, and Humorous—A New Selection*. London and New York: Burns & Oates, n.d. and other sources.

Judson, Adoniram (1788-1850). His Tender Side.

Judson is often called America's first missionary to foreign lands. He was in fact one of several sent forth at the same time. His cruel sufferings and those of his sacrificial wife Anne, made them household names in America. Through great perseverance and renunciation he translated the scriptures into Burmese and planted a church. Judson had a gentle side, described by his third wife, Emily Chubbuck. "He was always planning little surprises for family and neighbors, and kept through his married life those little lover-like attentions which I believe husbands are apt to forget." Here is an anecdote from his son exemplifying this tender-heartedness.

THE LITTLE THOUGHTFUL ATTENTIONS which he was continually paying to his fellow-missionaries, betrayed with what heartiness he entered into all their joys and sorrows. His friends, the Bennetts, had sent their children to America. One day Mr. Judson surprised them with a present of the portraits of their absent little ones, for which he had himself sent to this country.

- Judson, Edward. *Adoniram Judson*. Philadelphia: American Baptist Publication Society, 1894.

Kagawa, Toyohiko (1888-1960). Mad with Love.

After a near brush with death, Kagawa abandoned seminary to work among the poor in a Japanese slum. He pleaded for social justice and active faith: "Let him who would meet God visit the prison cell before going to the temple. Before he goes to church let him visit the hospital. Before he reads his Bible let him help the beggar standing at his door." He believed a Christian should be mad with love for God and men.

A BEGGAR REQUESTED his shirt, declaring that if Kagawa failed to hand it over, his Christianity would be shown up as a fraud. Kagawa gave the shirt. The next day the beggar returned and demanded the Christian's coat and trousers. Kagawa gave them as well. A sympathetic neighbor lady, virtually destitute herself, gave  him a kimono with a bright red lining. Kagawa and his red-streaked kimono became the laugh of all who saw him.

- Retold from William Axling's *Kagawa*. New York: Harper and Brothers, 1932.

Kelly, John (1750-1809). Saying...and Doing.

John Kelly, a graduate of Cambridge, served in the church of England, and was notable for his grammar, dictionary and Bible translation into the language of Manx (an ancient form of Gaelic found on the Isle of Man).

THE REV. MR. KELLY, curate of the English chapel in the town of Ayr, once preached an excellent sermon on the good Samaritan. He was particularly severe upon the conduct of the priest who saw the battered man, but passed on the opposite side.

"What!" he exclaimed, "not even the servant of the Almighty! he whose tongue was engaged in the word of charity, whose bosom was appointed the seat of brotherly love, whose heart the emblem of pity, whose soul the frozen serpent of disease! did he refuse to stretch forth his hand, and to take the mantle from his shoulders to cover the nakedness of woe? if he refused, if the shepherd himself went astray, was it to be wondered that the flock followed?"

Such were the precepts of this preacher, and he "practiced what he preached." The next day, when the river was rising, a boy in a small boat was swept overboard by the force of the current. A great crowd gathered, but none of them attempted to save the child. Rev. Kelly, seeing it all, although dressed in his heavy canonicals, threw himself from his window into the current, and at the risk of his own life saved the boy.

- Adapted from Sholto and Reuben Percy. *The Percy Anecdotes.* Harper & Brothers, 1847.

Ken, Thomas (1637-1711). Crossing the King.

Whether you know it or not, you may often have sung a hymn selection by Thomas Ken. A bishop and poet in the seventeenth century (and the close friend of angler Izaak Walton), he composed morning and evening prayers, both of which contain the refrain we know as the doxology: "Praise God from whom all blessings flow..." *Of the many volumes he filled with verse, those two hymns remain the only pieces we cherish. Ken is also noted for having boldly rebuked three of England's kings: Charles II, James II and William III. One of those rebukes and its outcome is told here.*

KING CHARLES II OF ENGLAND could not separate himself from the two mistresses who were then highest in his favor, the Duchess of Portsmouth and Nell Gwyn, and they had to be provided for. The official known as the "harbinger," to whose functions it belonged to  assign lodgings for the several members of the court, fixed on Ken's prebendal house for Nell. He probably assumed that one who had been recently appointed as a court chaplain would be subservient after the manner of his kind. With Ken, as we might expect, it was quite otherwise. He met the message with an indignant refusal. "A woman of ill-repute ought not to be endured in the house of a clergyman, least of all in that of the king's chaplain." Not for his kingdom would he comply with the king's demands. A local tradition relates that he took a practical way of settling the matter, by putting his house into a builder's hands and having it reroofed. Mrs. Eleanor Gwyn was, however, at last provided for. Dean Meggot was more compliant than the prebendary.

In the common calculations as to court favor, Ken risked his chance of future promotion by this act of boldness. Actually, he rose in Charles' esteem. Despite his profligacy, the king had not yet lost the power of recognizing goodness. The bold faithfulness of Ken as a preacher at Whitehall had led the king to say, in words which were remembered afterwards, as he was on his way to the royal closet, "I must go hear little Ken tell me of my faults." The courage which the chaplain now showed led the way, contrary to the expectations of all courtiers, to a fresh step onwards to the "great things" which Ken did not seek, but which were to be pressed upon him.

With the death of Bishop Morley of Winchester, the see of Winchester was filled by Peter Mews, Bishop of Bath and Wells, leaving Bath open. There were the usual floating rumors as to the see which he left vacant. Some talked of Dean Meggot, of Winchester, who had shown himself compliant in the matter of Nell Gwyn's lodgings; some of Parker, afterward Bishop of Oxford, and memorable in connection with the disputes between James II and the fellows of Magdalene College. Ken's name was also on the lips of men, since the king had been impressed by the sermons in which "little Ken tells me my faults." His work, as chaplain in the Tangier Expedition had also commended him, through Lord Dartmouth, to the notice of the Duke of York; and the Princess Mary was known to have formed a high estimate of his character. "Devout and honorable women" looked to him as the guide of their spiritual life. The only charge that was whispered against him was that he looked too favorably on the Church of Rome, and this with the king and his brother was, of course, not likely to be regarded as a drawback.

According to the current tradition of the time, however, Ken owed his advancement to that which, in the eyes of courtiers, would have seemed most likely to hinder it. When men were applying to him on behalf of this or that candidate, Charles is said to have stopped their representations with the declaration, "Odd's fish! Who shall have Bath and Wells but the little black fellow who would not give poor Nelly a lodging?" Ken's own friends were told that they need not trouble themselves; that "Dr. Ken should succeed, but that he designed it should be his own peculiar appointment." The rapidity with which the whole matter was decided is shown by the fact that, Morley having died on October 29th, Sunderland wrote, on November 4th, to Mews, to tell Ken that the king had nominated him for Winchester, and on the same day Arlington wrote to another of the king's chaplains, informing him that he was to be in attendance in the following February, "in the place of Dr. Ken, who is removed to be Bishop." Charles showed in this, as in some other instances, that he had not lost the power of respecting in others the goodness which he did not pretend to strive after for himself.

- E. H. Plumptre. *The Life of Thomas Ken, D.D., Bishop of Bath and Wells.* New York: E. & J. B. Young & Co., 1888.

Ketcham, Robert T. (1889-1978). Discovers God's Love.

Ketcham was raised in a Christian home, but marched out of it at 16 rather than abide by its rules. For several years he lived as a neer-do-well. After he converted, his life showed little change for over a year. He still frittered long hours in pool halls and smoking. However, the stubborn streak which took him from home at 16 eventually made him a founder of the General Association of Regular Baptist Churches. A key step in turning his stubbornness to God's use took place one night when he challenged a speaker at a Bible conference.

IN 1911 W. W. RUGH held a one week Bible conference at Galeton Baptist Church, Pennsylvania in which he explained the symbolism of the tabernacle. Ketcham was attracted by a big chart depicting the tent of worship which Rugh set up at the front of the church. Night after night he forsook the pool hall to listen to the speaker.

On the third night, Rugh declared that God loves each Christian just as much as he loves Jesus. To Ketcham that sounded like blasphemy. He waited for one of the elders or deacons to speak up, but no one did. The next night, Rugh declared that God had given every believer the same standing as Christ.

This was too much for Ketcham. When none of the church leaders stood up to refute a statement that seemed just plain wrong, he jumped to his feet and shouted, "Mr. Rugh, I don't believe that!"

Rugh smiled warmly at him. "You don't?" he asked.

Ketcham repeated his statement and said he also did not believe what Rugh had said the night before. Rugh asked him if he would believe it if he could show him from the Bible. Ketcham said he would.

Rugh (knowing full well the boy had no Bible) gave him a passage to look up: John 17:23. He brought his own Bible to the boy and Ketcham, who did not know where to look fumbled for several minutes. Finally Rugh helped him find the passage. Ketcham read, "I in them, and You in me, that they may be made perfect in one; and that the world may know that You have sent me, and have loved them, as You have loved me." Rugh also had him look at Ephesians 1:6 which teaches that we are accepted in the beloved—Christ.

The impact on Ketcham was astonishing. Realizing that God accepted him just as he accepted his own dear son, he sank into a pew and sobbed aloud. The whole church cried with him, suddenly aware of a truth they had never fully grasped either. After he regained control of himself, Ketcham prayed out loud, dedicating himself completely to the God who loved him so dearly.

- Adapted from Murdoch, J. Murray. *Portrait of Obedience; the biography of Robert T. Ketcham.* Schaumburg, Illinois: Regular Baptist Press, 1979.

Kimbrough, Isaac Barton (1826-1902). Retorting on a Pair of Robbers.

A frontier pastor in Tennessee and Texas, Kimbrough brought thousands to the Lord and served as a fundraiser for Carson and Newman College in his native Tennessee. Kimbrough pleaded for funds so diligently that he became known as "the beggar." How persuasive he could be is shown in this episode.

A PAIR OF HIGHWAYMEN pulled a gun on Kimbrough and ordered him to hand over his money. The fundraiser requested a moment to comply, dismounted from his horse, emptied the money from his pockets and laid it in two separate piles. He then told the robbers that the smallest pile was his. *That* they could take. However, he warned them the larger pile was the Lord's, and he dared them to touch it, explaining he had gathered it for the struggling young preachers of Carson and Newman College.

After learning he was a preacher and his mission, the men backed off from taking either pile of money. Kimbrough then turned the tables on them. He warned them they were in a bad line of business and pleaded with them to donate something to the school! Both robbers did.

• I first encountered this story in one of David L. Cummins' *This Day in Baptist History* series.

Knox, John (1514-1572). Lesson for Court Ladies.

John Knox was the reformer of Scotland and founder of the Presbyterian church.

WHEN KNOX SPOKE OUT against Queen Mary's proposed marriage to Don Carlos of Spain, she summoned him to court and vowed revenge.

After she had dried her passionate tears, she asked him, cuttingly, "What have you to do with my marriage? Or what are you within this Commonwealth?"

To this, Knox gave his memorable reply: "A subject born within the same, Madam!"

The queen cried some more and ordered him out of her private chamber into the broad court. There he stood, ignored and avoided as if he had the plague. Ladies drew their skirts back as they passed. Suddenly, in a powerful voice he cried out, "O fair ladies, how pleasing were this life of yours, if it could last, and in the end we might pass to heaven with all these showy clothes. But shame upon that knave Death, who will come whether we want or not! And when he has laid on his arrest, the foul worms will be busy with the flesh, be it ever so fair and so tender; and the silly soul I fear shall be so feeble, that it can neither carry with it gold, garnish, fringes, pearls, or precious stones..."

- Retold and adapted into modern English from Elizabeth Whitley's *Plain Mr. Knox*. London: Skeffington, 1960.

Kuyper, Abraham (1837-1920). Portrait of a Peasant.

The Dutch educator and statesman Abraham Kuyper was likened to a Renaissance man because of his vast knowledge and wide ability.

ABRAHAM KUYPER KEPT A PICTURE of a peasant woman named Pietje Baltus on his desk from about 1863 onward. Here is why: When he became minister of the Dutch Reformed Church in Beesd, he was a modernist without faith in Christ. Indeed, he even applauded a theologian who denied the resurrection. Pietje took him to task for not preaching the true Gospel. Kuyper found that she, and other peasants, were quite able to hold their own in theological arguments with him, despite his vast erudition. To his credit, he listened to them, and through the influence of their faith and prayers became a Christian.

When he left Beesd in 1867, he confessed to his congregation that he had begun his work there with an empty heart. He went on to labor his whole life for the restoration of living faith throughout the Netherlands and to apply scriptural principles to his nation's policies.

- These facts are stated more fully in James E. McGoldrick's *Abraham Kuyper: God's Renaissance Man*. Auburn, Massachusetts: Evangelical Press, 2000.

Lassenius, John (died 1692). Playing the Fool.

John Lassenius was a chaplain at the Danish court in the seventeenth century.

HAVING FOR A LONG TIME perceived to his vexation, that during his sermon, most of his congregation fell asleep, John Lassenius suddenly stopped one day, pulled a shuttlecock from his pocket, and began to play with it in the pulpit. Naturally this extraordinary behavior attracted the attention of those who were still awake. They jogged those who were sleeping, and in a short time everybody was lively, and looking to the pulpit with the greatest astonishment. This was just what Lassenius wished; for he immediately began to harangue them severely, saying, "When I announce to you sacred and important truths, you are not ashamed to go to sleep: but when I play the fool, you are all eye and all ear."

- Adapted from Sholto and Reuben Percy. *The Percy Anecdotes*. Harper & Brothers, 1847.

Latimer, Hugh (ca. 1485-1555). King vs. King.

Hugh Latimer was a beloved and godly English reformer who perished at the stake under Queen Mary. Here we see him in a famous act of courage.

UPON A CERTAIN OCCASION, when preaching before Henry, Hugh, as was his custom, spoke his mind very plainly, and the sermon displeased his Majesty; he was therefore commanded to preach again on the next Sabbath, and to make an apology for the offense he had given. After reading his text, the bishop began his sermon this way: "Hugh Latimer, do you know before whom you are this day to speak? To the high and mighty monarch, the king's most excellent majesty, who can take away your life if you offend; therefore take heed that you don't say a word that may displease! But then consider well, Hugh, don't you know where you come from and upon whose message you are sent? Even by the great and mighty God, who is all present, and who beholds all your ways, and who is able to cast your soul into hell! Therefore, take care that you deliver your message faithfully."

He then proceeded with the same sermon he had preached the preceding Sabbath, but with considerably more energy. The sermon ended, the court were full of expectation to know what would be the fate of this honest and plain-dealing bishop. After dinner, the king called for Latimer, and with a stern countenance asked him how he dared preach in such a manner. He, falling on his knees, replied his duty to his God and his prince had forced him to it, and that he had merely discharged his duty and cleared his conscience by what he had spoken. Upon which the king, rising from his seat, and taking the good man by the hand, embraced him, saying, "Blessed be God, I have so honest a servant."

- Adapted from Charles Spurgeon. *Eccentric Preachers*. London: Passmore and Alabaster, 1879.

Leland, John (1506-1552). Destruction of Irreplaceable Books

John Leland was the father of English local history, making the shire the basic unit of study; and he was also a chaplain to King Henry VIII.

HENRY GAVE A COMMISSION to the famous antiquary, John Leland, to examine the libraries of the suppressed religious houses, and preserve whatever touched on history. Though Leland, after his search, told the king he had "conserved many good authors, which otherwise had been likely to have perished, to the no small incommodity of good letters," he acknowledged the ruthless destruction of all such as were connected with various doctrines of the Roman Catholic church. John Strype, an English historian of the following century, noted with great sorrow that many ancient manuscripts and writings of learned British and Saxon authors were lost. Mercenary men sold entire libraries for anything they could get following the devastation of the religious houses. Bale, an antiquary, mentioned a merchant who bought two noble libraries about this time for forty shillings; whose books served him for no other use but for waste paper; and noted that after he had been ten years consuming them, there remained enough for as many more years. Vast quantities of these books vanished with the monks and friars from their monasteries, were conveyed away and carried over seas to booksellers by the shipfull; and a great many more were used in shops and kitchens.

- Adapted from Isaac D'Israeli's *Curiosities of Literature*. London: Frederick and Warne, 1881.

Leland, John (1754-1841). A Gift for President Thomas Jefferson.

John Leland was a well-known Baptist evangelist in his day and author of the hymn "The Day Is Past and Gone."

THE MUCH PERSECUTED BAPTISTS of the United States were deeply grateful to Thomas Jefferson, who, before becoming president, had been a champion of their religious rights. In 1801, they determined to send him a gift to show their appreciation and delegated evangelist John Leland to deliver it.

He set out from Massachusetts in November and delivered the gift on January 1st, 1802, having preached the whole way to crowds who gathered to see the unusual gift. Jefferson received the present graciously and invited Leland to visit the senate with him. And what was the gift? A giant cheese, weighing 900 pounds made by the women of Cheshire, Massachusetts.

- Derived from internet sources and Reuben Herring's *The Baptist Almanac and Repository of Indispensable Knowledge*. Nashville, Tennessee: Broadman Press, 1976.

Lewis, C. S. (1898-1963). A Shaky Kayak Ride; Substitution.

C. S. Lewis was a twentieth-century Christian apologist, scholar, teacher, and author.

A shaky kayak ride. IN HIS AUTOBIOGRAPHY, *Lenten Lands,* Douglas Gresham (whose mother, Joy, married C. S. Lewis), gives several instances of Lewis' compassion and understanding, including this: Douglas had been given a kayak which he paddled around the lake behind their home. While he was still unsteady, Lewis hailed him and asked for a ride across the lake. Nervously, Douglas obliged, fearing he might tip "Jack" into the cold water. Lewis praised Douglas and his craft. Douglas wrote, "I glowed in the warmth of his praise and approval, for by then I loved and respected Jack and to win his approbation gave me a rush of happiness. Jack risked a ducking in a cold lake simply to please a rather too cocksure boy because he knew that in so doing he would make both me and Mother very happy."

- Retold from Douglas H. Gresham's *Lenten Lands.* New York: Macmillan Publishing co., 1988; p. 110.

Substitution. NOT LONG AFTER HER MARRIAGE to C. S. Lewis, Joy Gresham developed cancer. Expected to die, she came home from the hospital to the Kilns in 1957. Lewis, acting on a theory of substitution advanced by his friend Charles William, prayed at length that he might take some of Joy's pain on himself.

"The results were astonishing," wrote biographer George Sayers. Joy improved that April but Lewis came down with a painful osteoporosis in midsummer, a disease in which the bones are weakened through calcium loss.

While Joy, who desperately needed it, was gaining calcium in her bones, he was losing it from his. Lewis commented later, "One dreams of a Charles Williams' substitution!"

- Retold from George Sayers. *Jack; C. S. Lewis and His Times*. San Francisco: Harper & Row, 1988; p. 225. This also appears in Sheldon Vanauken's *A Severe Mercy*. New York: Bantam, 1981.

Linley, Ozias (1765-1831). Shinny Down a Drain Pipe.

Rev. Linley was notorious for drifting into deep thought and forgetting what he was supposed to be doing. Below is a story he told on himself.

"IT WAS MY TURN," said Rev. Linley, "as a minor canon, to preach in Norwich Cathedral, and well knowing my own infirmity [forgetfulness], I rang the bell, and put the key of my study into my landlady's hands, requesting her to lock the door, and come again to let me out in time for the service. She raised objections, and insisted on returning the key, but somehow I remained under an impression she had taken it with her as I desired. Accordingly I read my sermon over till the bells began to ring. I then put on my surplice, but no landlady came to release me. I read half my sermon over again, but still no landlady appeared. Looking out of the window, I saw the congregation assembling, and at length the great bell began to toll, as it always did when the Dean and Chapter were about to form into procession. Still no landlady appeared. In this extremity, I threw open the window, and with the help of the water-butt and water-spout, climbed down in my canonicals into the street. Happily I was so late that comparatively few of the congregation witnessed this exploit. On my return home after the service, I put my hand mechanically into my pocket, and had opened the door of my lodgings before I called to mind my imaginary difficulty.

- W. Davenport Adams. *Modern Anecdotes; a treasury of wise and witty sayings of the last hundred years.* London, Hamilton, Adams, 1886.

Livingston, John of Ancrum (1603-1672). A Sermon He Wanted to Run From.

John Livingstone was a Scottish Covenanter, the son of a minister. A Christian from his infancy, he planned to become a lawyer, but after a day alone in a cave seeking God's purpose, he determined to become a preacher. He proved to be a conscientious one. In the course of years, he was twice forced to flee to the continent.

WHEN IN 1625 he began to speak for his Master, he had his first taste of persecution. Congregations in different parts—Torphichen, Linlithgow, Leith, Kirkcaldy—were eager to claim him; but in each case the bishops prevented the settlement. For five years he had no sphere of work peculiarly his own. But God's blessing went with him through the period of waiting.

Sometimes the preaching of the Covenanters is condemned as cold and hard; but Livingston's words had the flame of the Holy Ghost glowing in them, and they conquered and captivated the souls of men. One of the great revivals in the annals of the Church is linked with the name of the young probationer whom the bishops pursued with hate.

It happened at the Kirk of Shotts, on the 21st of June 1630, a Monday. With some friends he had spent the previous night laying fast hold upon the promise and the grace of Heaven. When the midsummer morning broke, the preacher wanted to escape from the responsibilities in front of him. Alone in the fields, between eight and nine, he felt such misgivings, such a burden of unworthiness, such dread of the crowd and their expectations, that he actually considered creeping away from the task; but he dared not "so far distrust God;" and so he went to the sermon, "and got good assistance."

Good assistance indeed! After he had spoken for an hour and a half from the text, "Then will I sprinkle clean water upon you, and you shall be clean," and was thinking that now he must close, he was constrained by the Lord Himself to continue.

"I was led on about one hour's time in a strain of exhortation and warning, with such liberty and melting of heart as I never had the like in public all my life." No fewer than 500 men and women, some of them ladies of high estate, and others poor wastrels and beggars, traced the dawn of eternal life in their souls to John Livingston's words that day.

- Adapted from Alexander Smellie's *Men of the Covenant; the story of the Scottish church in the years of the persecution.* London: Melrose, 1903.

Lombard Churches (1059). Reluctant Submission.

The Roman church had competition from other churches (such as the Orthodox and Celtic churches, and the Waldenses) during periods of the Middle Ages. Italy's Lombardy region resisted control by Rome into the eleventh century. At that time, Milan still used the liturgy of Ambrose, and much of the region had been uplifted by two reform-minded bishops—Claude of Turin and Vigilantius (who rejected relics, the worship of saints, the elevation of the unmarried state and other practices which were in common use). Rome continued to renew its attempts to induce the bishops of Milan to accept the palladium, a token of spiritual vassalage to the pope, but not until 1059, under Nicholas II, was it successful.

THE PONTIFF DISPATCHED Petrus Damianus, bishop of Ostia, and Anselm, bishop of Lucca, to receive the submission of the Lombard churches. In places, the people came close to rioting in their unwillingness to accept this submission. The clergy, too, showed that they were unhappy at the idea of submitting to Rome. Damianus wrote that the clergy of Milan maintained in his presence "that the Ambrosian Church, according to the ancient institutions of the Fathers, was always free, without being subject to the laws of Rome, and that the Pope of Rome had no jurisdiction over their church as to the government or constitution of it."

- Adapted from J. A. Wylie's *History of the Waldenses*. Washington, D.C. Review and Herald Publishing Association, ca. 1880.

Louis IX of France (1215-1270). Rejects a Fate Different than His People.

St. Louis IX, King of France, was crowned king at eleven years of age. It is doubtful any other Medieval French king was as saintly, beloved, or revered. Here is one incident demonstrating his character.

LOUIS IX, after his captivity among the Saracens, was, with his queen and children, nearly shipwrecked on his return to France, some of the planks of the vessel having loosened. He was pressed to go on board another ship, and so escape the danger, but he refused, saying, "Those that are with me, most assuredly are as fond of their lives as I can be of mine. If I leave the ship, they will likewise leave it; and the other not being large enough to receive them, they will all perish. I had rather entrust my life, and the lives of my wife and children, in the hands of God, than be the occasion of making so many of my brave subjects suffer."

- *The Book of Three Hundred Anecdotes Historical, Literary, and Humorous—A New Selection.* London and New York: Burns & Oates, n.d.

Luther, Martin (1483-1546). Father and Children.

Apart from our Lord and the individuals mentioned in the New Testament, Martin Luther is the best-known individual in church history. The highlights of his life are well-known: the lightening strike that drove him into a monastery; tacking up the 95 theses to the Wittenberg church door; his stand before rulers; his kidnap; his marriage to an escaped nun; his refusal to shake Zwingli's hand. Let us pass these by and look at another area, less well known, but greatly influential— his relationship with children. Who can measure the influence he had on family life or the elevation he brought to the rearing of the young?

WITH REGARD TO HIS CHILDREN, Luther resolved from the moment of their birth to consecrate them to God, and wean them from a wicked, corrupt, and accursed world. In several of his letters he entreats his friends with great earnestness to stand godfather to one of his children, and to help the poor little heathen to become Christian, and pass from death of sin to a holy and blessed regeneration. In making this request of a young Bohemian nobleman, then staying in his house, in behalf of his son Martin, he grew so earnest that, to the surprise of all present, his voice trembled; this, he said, was caused by the Holy Spirit of God, for the cause he was pleading was God's and it demanded reverence. And yet, in the simple, natural, innocent and happy ways of children, he recognized the precious handiwork of God and His protecting hand. He loved to watch the games and pleasures of his little ones; all they did was so spontaneous and so natural, Children, he said, believe so simply and undoubtedly that God is in Heaven and is their God and their dear Father and that there is everlasting life. On hearing one day one of his children prattling about this life and of the great joy in Heaven with eating, and dancing, and so forth, he said, "Their life is the most blessed and the best; they have none but pure thoughts and happy imaginations." At the sight of his little children seated round the table, he called to mind the exhortation of Jesus, that we must "become as little children;" and added, "Ah, dear God! Thou hast done clumsily in exalting children—such poor little simpletons—so high. Is it just and right that You should reject the wise and receive the foolish? But God our Lord has purer thoughts than we have; He must therefore refine us...He must hew great boughs and chips from us, before He makes such children and little simpletons of us."......

Luther warned against all outbursts of passion and undue severity toward children, and carefully guarded himself against such errors, remembering the bitter experiences of his own childhood in that respect. But he could be angry and strict enough when the occasion required; he used to say he would rather have a dead son than a bad one.

There was no really good school at Wittenberg for his boys, and Luther could not devote as much time to them as they required. He took a resident tutor for them, a young theologian. His boy John nonetheless gave some trouble with his teaching and bringing up. His father, contrary to his own wishes, seems to have been too weak, and his mother's fondness for her first-born seems to have somewhat spoilt him. Luther gave the boy over afterward to his friend Mark Crodel, the Rector of the school of Torgau, whom he held in high respect as a grammarian, and as a pedagogue of grave and strict morals.

His favorite child was little Lena, a pious, gentle, affectionate little girl, and devoted to him with her whole heart. A charming picture of her remains, by Cranach, a friend of the family. But she died in the bloom of early youth, on September 20, 1542, after a long and severe illness. The grief he had felt at the loss of his daughter Elizabeth was now renewed and intensified. When she was lying on her sick-bed, he said, "I love her very much indeed, but, dear God, if it is Your will to take her from here, I would be glad she was with You." To Magdalene herself he said, "Lena, my dear little daughter, you would love to remain here with your father; are you willing to go to that other Father?"

"Yes, dear father," she answered; "Just as God wills." And when she was dying, he fell on his knees beside her bed, wept bitterly, and prayed for her redemption, and she fell asleep in his arms.

As she lay in her coffin, he looked at her and exclaimed, "Ah! my darling Lena, you will rise again and shine like a star—yes, as the sun;" and added, "I am happy in the spirit, but in the flesh I am very sorrowful. The flesh will not be subdued: parting troubles one above measure; it is a wonderful thing to think that she is assuredly in peace, and that all is well with her, and yet to be so sad." To the mourners he said, "I have sent a saint to heaven: could mine be such a death as hers, I would welcome such a death this moment." He expressed the same sorrow, and the same exultation in his letters to his friends. To Jonas he wrote: "You will have heard that my dearest daughter Magdalene is born again in the everlasting kingdom of Christ. Although I and my wife ought only to thank God with joy for her happy departure, whereby she has escaped the power of the world, the flesh, the Turks and the devil, yet so strong is natural love that we cannot bear it without sobs and sighs from the heart, without a bitter sense of death in ourselves. So deeply printed on our hearts are her ways, her words, her gestures, whether alive or dying, that even Christ's death cannot drive away this agony." His little Hans, whom his sister longed to see once more, he had sent for from Torgau a fortnight before she died: he wrote for that purpose to Crodel, saying, "I would not have my conscience reproach me afterward for having neglected anything." But when several weeks later, about Christmas-time, under the influence of grief and the tender words which his mother had spoken to him, a desire came over the boy to leave Torgau and live at home, his father exhorted him to conquer his sorrow like a man, not to increase by his own the grief of his mother, and to obey God, who had appointed him, through his parents' direction, to live at Torgau.

- Julius Kostlin. *Life of Luther*. New York: Scribner's Sons, 1884.

McCheyne, Robert Murray (1813-1843). Gentleness. Godliness.

Robert Murray McCheyne was a gentle and godly preacher and revival leader who died at the young age of 29, deeply mourned in Scotland. His collected writings, consisting of sermons and letters, have gone through hundreds of editions.

His gentleness. MCCHEYNE WAS CAREFUL never to speak with bitterness. He well understood that some pastors use God's word to bully and frighten their listeners; and said of the Gospel, "Surely it is a gentle message, and should be spoken with angelic tenderness, especially by such a needy sinner."

Once, upon meeting up with a fellow pastor he asked what his last sermon had been on. The other man replied that he had preached on the text, The wicked shall be turned into hell.

McCheyne immediately asked with concern of this fearsome text, "Were you able to preach it with tenderness?"

- Adapted from S. Maxwell Coder's biographical introduction to Andrew A. Bonar's *Memoirs of McCheyne; including his letters and messages*. Chicago: Moody Press, 1947.

His godliness. ONE WOMAN who heard McCheyne preach exclaimed afterwards, "When, in his prayer, I heard him say, 'O

Lord, Thou knowest that we love Thee!" I felt that I would gladly give all that I hoped to possess to be able to say that to the Savior."

- Quoted in F. W. Boreham's *Lake Lark Ascending*. London: Epworth Press, 1945.

McDowell, Josh (1939-). Impossible "Coincidence" Clears Concern.

Josh McDowell was an evangelist in Campus Crusade and author of several apologetics books including Evidence that Demands a Verdict.

JOSH MCDOWELL REACHED A POINT at which he could hardly eat or sleep because of his distress to know whether his dead mother had ever become a Christian. He saw no way to discover the facts because so much time had passed. At the time when this concern came upon him, he was in California. He prayed that God would somehow answer his question: had his mother been saved or not? "Please, I've just got to know."

Two days later, he visited a beach. It was chilly. As he stood there, a woman, who looked old enough to be his grandmother, spoke to him. They exchanged pleasantries and she found out he was from Union City, Michigan. The woman knew the place. "I had a cousin from there," she said. "Do you know the McDowell family?"

It turned out Josh was speaking to Mrs. Bowder, a cousin who had grown up with his mother in Idaho. Bowder was a Christian. Josh asked her if she remembered anything about his mother's spiritual life. She did. The two had asked the Lord into their hearts on the same evening in a camp meeting.

Thus God answered McDowell's "impossible" prayer in the most improbable manner within 72 hours.

- Derived from the account in Joe Musser's *A Skeptics Quest; Josh McDowell's Search for Reality.* San Bernardino, California: Here's Life Publishers, 1984; pp. 79-82.

Maillard, Oliver (died 1502). Satire to Offend a King.

Oliver Maillard was a witty Franciscan preacher of fifteenth century France, the author of many sermons which are still extant.

OLIVER MAILLARD, a French doctor of divinity, having pointed some sharp comments at King Louis XI, irritated that cruel monarch. Servants of the king informed the preacher that if he continued in this vein, he would soon find himself thrown into the river. He replied, "The king may do as he chooses; but tell him that I shall sooner get to paradise by water, than he will arrive by all his post-horses." He alluded to traveling by post, which this monarch had lately introduced into France. Apparently this bold answer intimidated Louis, for Maillard continued as courageous and satirical as ever in his pulpit—but not in the river.

- Adapted from Isaac D'Israeli's *Curiosities of Literature.* London: Frederick and Warne, 1881.

Marshall, Daniel (1706-1784). Words that Stuck.

Farmer-preacher Daniel Marshall was not a great speaker, but God used him to found 18 Baptist churches and to form Baptist associations in North and South Carolina and in Georgia. At that time, Baptists were frequently persecuted by the established church and civil authorities, and Daniel came in for his share.

SHERIFF SAMUEL CARTLEDGE arrested Daniel Marshall near Augusta, Georgia while Marshall was on his knees praying. Marshall warned Cartledge that he needed to be saved from his sins, but the sheriff proceeded with the arrest. The magistrate, Colonel Barnard, forbade Marshall to preach in Georgia again. Marshall's obedience to Christ, however, made a lasting impact on both men. His warning stuck with Cartledge. Six years later it bore fruit when the sheriff came for Marshall again—this time to seek baptism from him. The sheriff became a Baptist minister. In the course of time, the magistrate also became an earnest Christian.

- Derived from the *New Georgia Encyclopedia* and Reuben Herring's *The Baptist Almanac and Repository of Indispensable Knowledge.* Nashville, Tennessee: Broadman Press, 1976 and internet articles.

Matthews, Katherine (Seventeenth Century). Ultimate Aim.

Katherine Matthews became the wife of Philip Henry and mother of the famous Bible commentator Matthew Henry.

WHEN PHILIP HENRY came as pastor to Worthenbury, Wales, he fell in love with Katherine Matthews and she returned his affection. Her father, a wealthy landowner, was not happy at the prospect of a penniless preacher for a son-in-law.

He tried to argue his daughter out of the match, pointing out that, however good a preacher Henry was, she knew very little about him. "Why, we don't even know where he came from!"

"That may be," retorted his witty daughter, "but I know where he is going, and I should like to go with him."

- This anecdote appears in slightly different forms in F. W. Boreham's *A Late Lark Singing*. London: Epworth, 1945; and in Walter Baxendale's *Dictionary of Anecdote, Incident, Illustrative Fact*. New York: Thomas Whittaker, 1889.

Melville, Andrew (1545-1622). Covenanter Accepts the King's Dare.

Andrew Melville was a scholarly and zealous pastor in Scotland who refused to accept the system of bishops King James wished to impose on the church. His belief that he was acting on Biblical principles made him so bold he even grabbed the king by the sleeve once to remonstrate with him, and on another occasion told the king he was "God's silly vassal."

KING JAMES I of Great Britain, VI of Scotland, aspired to rule the Scots Church. The General Assembly resisted his claim, sending a delegation to the king with a strong remonstrance against his tyrannical course. Melville was a member of the delegation, and his energetic spirit made him their speaker. The delegation appeared in the royal court where James sat among his advisers. The remonstrance was read; it filled the king with rage. "Who dares subscribe this treasonable paper?" was asked.

"We dare," replied Melville, taking hold of the pen and calmly writing his name. The others followed his bold example. The king and his company were overawed by their holy bravery.

- Adapted from J. C. McFeeters' *Sketches of the Covenanters*. Public domain.

Middleton (died 1548). A Prophetic Warning.

Under Edward VI, Anabaptists were martyred. In 1548, English authorities arrested four of their ministers, Hart, Middleton, Coal, and Brodbridge.

MIDDLETON WAS MARTYRED in the reign of Edward, and when Archbishop Cranmer threatened him with death he replied, "Reverend Sir, pass what sentence you think fit upon us. But that you may not say that you were not forewarned, I testify that your turn may be next." Eight years afterward, this expectation was realized, when Cranmer himself burned.

- Adapted from Thomas Armitage's *A History of the Baptists traced by their Vital Principles and Practices from the Time of Our Lord and Savior Jesus Christ to the Year 1886.* New York: Bryan, Taylor & Co., 1887.

Moffat, Robert (1795-1883). Welcomes Hottentots.

Robert Moffat was almost rejected by his mission society which doubted he had the stuff to succeed. However, he became a notable missionary to South Africa, and the father-in-law of David Livingstone.

IT HAPPENED ONE EVENING, soon after I began my journey up the country, that I found my way to the homestead of a Dutch Boer, of whom I begged a night's lodging. It was nightfall and the family must soon go to rest. But first would the stranger address some words of Christian counsel to them? Gladly I assented and the big barn was resorted to. Looking round on my congregation, I saw my host and hostess with their family. There were crowds of black forms hovering near at hand, but never a one was there in the barn. I waited, hoping they might be coming. But no, no one came. Still I waited as expecting something.

"What ails you," said the farmer. "Why don't you begin?"

"May not your servants come too?" I replied.

"Servants!" shouted the master. "Do you mean the Hottentots? Are you mad to think of preaching to the Hottentots? Go to the mountains and preach to the baboons; or if you like, I'll fetch my dogs, and you may preach to them!"

This was too much for my feelings, and the tears began to trickle down my cheeks. I opened my New Testament, and read out for my text the words, "Truth, Lord: yet the dogs eat the crumbs that fall from their master's table."

A second time the words were read, and then my host, vanquished by the arrow from God's own quiver, cried out, "Stop! You must have your own way. I'll get you all the Hottentots and they shall hear you."

The barn soon filled with rows of dark forms, whose eager looks gazed on the stranger. I then preached my first sermon to the heathen. I shall never forget that night.

- Walter Baxendale's *Dictionary of Anecdote, Incident, Illustrative Fact.* New York: Thomas Whittaker, 1889.

Montgomery, James (1771-1854). Tender Conscience Dressed Runaway in Rags.

James Montgomery was a minor British poet of the nineteenth century, noted for his hymns and the carol "Angels We Have

Heard on High." He edited the Sheffield Iris *and was a leading philanthropist. As editor he was twice imprisoned—once for printing a poem deemed subversive, the second time for reporting a massacre that the government wanted covered up. This anecdote concerns his youth. When his mother and father sailed as Moravian missionaries to the West Indies, they left him in the care of Scots Brethren, who educated him and placed him with a shopkeeper. James, whose taste was for literature, ran away.*

BECOMING MORE AND MORE DISCONTENTED with this situation, so unsuitable to his taste and capabilities; and not being legally bound to his master by indentures of apprenticeship, one fine Sunday morning in June 1789, he packed up his few things, not forgetting above all his precious manuscript poetry, and set out to seek his fortune. "You will smile," says he, "and wonder, too, when I inform you that I was such as fool as to run away from my master with the clothes on my back, a single change of linen, and three-and-sixpence in my pocket. I had just got a new set of clothes; but as I had only been a short time with my good master, I did not think my little services had earned them. I therefore left him in my old ones; and thus, at the age of sixteen, set out James Montgomery to begin the world!"

As eyed by the passing traveler, what a figure he would cut! With spectacles on his nose, for he was nearsighted, his scholarly aspect would but ill assort with the old clothes in which he was clad; his conscience being so tender as to forbid him to don his new ones...

- Adapted from Samuel Ellis's *Life, Times and Character of James Montgomery*. London: Jackson, Walford & Hodder, 1864.

Moody, Dwight L. (1837-1899). Counterforce. Reading Character.

Dwight Moody was the most notable American evangelist of the nineteenth century.

Counterforce. ONE DAY while crossing the Connecticut River on a ferry, which was pulled across by a line stretched over the river, P.P. Bliss and Sankey were singing, "Pull for the shore, sailor, pull for the shore," when they noticed that the boat pulled unusually heavy; and on investigating, found that Moody, who was sitting in the rear, was pulling back on the line with all his might, so as to delay the trip, and give himself a chance to listen to the singing. Although himself not a singer, Moody used the service of praise more extensively and successfully than any other evangelist in the nineteenth century.

Reading character. OUR NEXT LARGE MEETINGS were held in Chicago during the fall of 1876, in a large Tabernacle erected for the occasion by John V. Farwell. It was capable of seating more than eight thousand. At one of these meetings Mr. Moody's attention was attracted by an usher with a wand in his hand, seating the people as they came in. Mr. Moody did not like the man's appearance. He asked the chairman of the committee, Mr. Harvey, who the usher was. Mr. Harvey replied that he did not know, but would go and see. Taking the man out into the inquiry room, Mr. Harvey learned that his name was Guiteau—the man who afterward shot President Garfield. So great was Mr. Moody's power in reading character.

- Both accounts are from Ira D. Sankey's *My Life and the Story of the Gospel Hymns*. Philadelphia: Sunday School Times, 1907.

Morgan, G. Campbell (1863-1945). The Power of Example.

G. Campbell Morgan, the son of a Baptist preacher, became a great evangelical preacher himself and wrote many books known for their fresh understanding of the scriptures.

THE CONVERSION of G. Campbell Morgan shows the importance of godly example. "While my father could not compel me to be a Christian, I had no choice because of what he did for me and what I saw in him."

- This quote is repeated in several biographical sketches of G. Morgan Campbell.

Neesima Shimeta (1843-1890). Effect of a Novel.

As a youth, Neesima Shimeta was fascinated by the west and believed that Japan would be destroyed by western powers if it did not understand western ways. Consequently he defied

Japanese law and left his homeland aboard an American ship in one of the ports open to foreign trade, although the penalty for doing so was death. Eventually, he returned to spread Christianity in Japan.

GOD TEACHES PEOPLE through unexpected means. When Neesima Shimeta eluded the ship inspectors and made his escape from Japan, he had already picked up some knowledge of world history and of Christianity through Dutch and Chinese sources. He was impressed with what he heard of the United States and made his way there to study. In Boston, he saw no way to proceed with his desire for an education, but began reading an English novel in order to improve his language skills. That novel taught him to pray.

It was *Robinson Crusoe,* by Daniel Defoe. In the story, hardships bring impious Crusoe to the point where he calls upon God for salvation. Defoe, who belonged to the Dissenters (those who separated from the established church in England), often used his vivid writings to score moral points. *Robinson Crusoe,* published in 1719, had leapfrogged 150 years to touch a Japanese life with faith.

- The incident is mentioned in Kenneth Scott Latourette. *These Sought a Country.* New York: Harper and Brothers, 1950 and in other accounts of Neesima.

Newton, John (1725-1807). Certainties; Finding God's Will.

Once a slaver, Newton was converted and became a pastor, the author of the popular hymn "Amazing Grace." The first anecdote shows his view of salvation, the second how he sought to be sure the Lord was calling him to the ministry.

All-sufficient Savior. JOHN NEWTON, on being asked his opinion on some subject, replied: "When I was young I was sure of many things; there are only two things of which I am sure now: one is, that I am a miserable sinner; and the other, that Jesus Christ is an all-sufficient savior."

- Walter Baxendale's *Dictionary of Anecdote, Incident, Illustrative Fact.* New York: Thomas Whittaker, 1889.

Finding God's Will. IT IS NOW ABOUT 8 MONTHS since the conversation of some friends, led my thoughts to the [ministry]. The first mention made little impression on me, but in a small time it took firmer hold of my mind; and at length found a place in my prayers so far only, as to profess my readiness to enter on that service, if the Lord should at any time see fit to call, prepare and send me. In a little time this submission to be employed, improved into a wish and desire that I might, which still continues and increases. I have many times in this interval given myself to the Lord for His service ... I hope without reserve or condition; and I referred myself to the time when I should be able to read a chapter in the Hebrew Bible with tolerable ease for a farther and close enquiry into this matter; in which I determined to join my own serious deliberations, the advice of my best and most judicious friends, and a course of prayer, and waiting upon the Lord.

By the divine blessing upon my studies I can now read a chapter etc, nearly in the manner I proposed. My birthday will return on the 4 August; I determine by the grace of God to set apart the 6 ensuing weeks to that day, I mean as much of my time as I can conveniently command, to wait upon the Lord, to examine my own heart, to consider at large the nature, dignity, difficulty and importance of the great undertaking I have in view; and if after this term, I find my mind still engaged to the work, I intend to dedicate the day of my entrance upon a new year of life (my 34th) to solemn fasting and prayer, in which I will endeavor to engage my dear Christian friends at London, Leeds etc, to concur with me. I then propose to give myself up anew to God, and do humbly pray and believe that He will in His good time and way let me know that He has accepted me; and will prevent me taking any hasty or disorderly steps, that may bring a reproach upon my profession or involve me in needless difficulties..."

Newton proceeded to set forth a number of resolves by which he would be guided and devoted several more days in his journal to meditations and considerations on the ministry, weighing God's word, and attempting to be sure it was a call from the Lord and not his own whim.

• John Newton. *Journal.*

Nida, Eugene (1914-). Boxing a Heckler.

A top linguist with the American Bible Society, Nida was responsible for training many missionaries in Bible translation, and directly or indirectly helping them produce versions of the Bible in hundreds of languages.

DURING A FIESTA IN MEXICO, a drunken man baited Nida repeatedly. Nida tolerated the annoyance for a reasonable length of time, but finally resorted to one of his non-linguistic skills. He had been a welterweight boxer in college, and to the delight of the Indians, he soon dealt with his heckler.

- Henry La Cossitt. "He Takes the Bible 'Round the World." *Colliers* (March 18, 1955) 56-7.

Norwich Baptists (Eighteenth Century). No Lottery.

IN THOSE DAYS, when the state churches of Connecticut wanted to build a meeting house, they commonly asked the legislature for a lottery grant on which to raise money. The Norwich Baptists, thinking it no harm for them to be as ridiculous as other respectable folk, applied to the General Assembly for such a grant. Whereupon that august body refused: first, because the Baptists did not endorse the ecclesiastical laws; secondly, because they were not known in law as a denomination; thirdly, because Rev. Mr. Sterry, the Baptist pastor at Norwich, was the co-editor of a Republican paper. For these reasons, our brethren were informed that they could not be allowed to gamble like good, legal and orthodox saints. This word to the wise had a wholesome effect upon them, for although they have now built a number of excellent church edifices, and have liberally helped others to do the same, they have never once since asked for a state lottery to help them in building houses for God.

- Adapted from Thomas Armitage's *A History of the Baptists Traced by their Vital Principles and Practices from the Time of Our Lord and Savior Jesus Christ to the Year 1886.* New York: Bryan, Taylor & Co., 1887.

Oberlin, John Frederick (1740-1826). Awkward Proposal.

Protestant pastor Jean Frederic Oberlin promoted the Gospel in a very poor area of northeastern France. Despite the peasants' initial suspicion, he convinced them to adopt practices which brought them prosperity. Among these were founding a savings and loan, building roads, introducing cotton manufactures, improving agricultural, and opening orphanages.

PREVIOUS TO HIS DEPARTURE to his mountain parish, Oberlin's mother, mindful of his welfare, advised him to take a wife with him to the parsonage. He had no such purpose for himself, but he was quite willing to be counseled in a matter beyond his contemplated plans. Believing that everything should be a matter of prayer, he committed this also to the Lord, but the two women his mother arranged for him to meet proved unsatisfactory.

Here ended the mother's endeavors to secure a fitting companion for her son. The question was settled, but Oberlin was not. His mother, however, could not consent to her son's departure alone. She accompanied him to Waldbach, settled him, unmarried, and left his younger sister Sophia in charge of his new home. Busy with the beginnings of his self-denying life among his poor people, he had neither time nor inclination to turn his thoughts to any further matrimonial experiments. Sister Sophia was all that his heart could wish in making a home a refuge from his cares.

Nevertheless, in that remote and lonely place it was to be expected that this sister Sophia would have many lonely hours, accustomed as she was to Strasbourg life; and when a year had been spent in this way, she induced her intimate friend, Madeline Witter, after a somewhat serious illness, to visit her and try the bracing mountain air for recuperation; this rather against the preferences of Oberlin. Witter, who was related to Oberlin on her mother's side, was the daughter of a former professor of the University of Strasbourg, but had lost both of her parents at an early age. She was now a well-educated city girl, with far more expensive habits than were approved by Oberlin, but charming and lively.

Oberlin's severe views of life and the nature of his work were such that the gaiety of the visit was not altogether agreeable to him, and he lost no occasion to express in a kindly way his little disagreements with her apparently less serious attitudes of thought and feeling. Madeline met his ironies with happy rejoinders; quick of wit, she was not second to him in repartee, and while neither of them thought it, they were coming to appreciate and enjoy each other in their perfect independence of opinions and ability to defend them. Then came an indication to Oberlin (shall we call it Providential?) such as he had not distinctly prayed for, that the gay, witty, charming young woman would be a delightful companion, a real comrade in life. As soon as he realized this he determined to resist the growing intimacy, giving to himself as reasons her joyous temperament, her over-elegant toilet, and her worldly habits. Nor was he unmindful of the declaration he had often heard her make, that she "would never marry a clergyman." The visit continued for some weeks, every day weaving the toils closer about them both. Oberlin, in his journal, confesses the conquest that had been made and recorded "two sleepless nights."

While Providence continued the intimations in this unsolicited way, the time came when the young lady's immediate departure was at hand. Repeatedly seeking divine guidance, the young pastor looked for signs to indicate God's will. It is recorded that he solemnly declared to God that if he would give him a sign, he would act accordingly. The only sign which came was "an inner voice that seemed to repeat, 'Take her for your wife.'" He replied to himself, "But it is impossible; our dispositions and our tastes are so dissimilar," and the inner voice reiterated, "Take her for your wife." That the wish was father to the voice is clear enough. The voice was as evidently a real one. It was the voice of his own heart, though Oberlin did not interpret it that way.

He decided at last that this was indeed the intimation of Providence, and then he lost no time in obeying the divine will. It was a glad obedience. He sought the lady under the shade of a tree which still stands in the garden, and how his declaration has come down to us in words I know not, but his original biographer and friend, who was assisted by Oberlin's daughter in handing down the romance, writes that Oberlin said: "You are about to leave us, my dear friend, but I have had an intimation that you are destined by divine will to be the partner of my life. If you will resolve upon this step, so important to us both, I expect you will give me your candid opinion about it before your departure."

Let us hope that his biographer and friend did not get correctly all that was said on this occasion, even if the young missionary may have been able to interweave these words into his declaration. We know that Oberlin was accustomed to enter in his diary his daily thoughts, and it is quite possible that in the cool of the evening with his pen in hand, in the mental reaction after such an experience, he thought that he made these identical remarks. At all events we may be sure that he asked this sweet girl, who had abundant humor and a sense of the ridiculous, to share his life in such a way that she did not laugh at its putting, and without concealing from her that a life of sacrifice, solitude and poverty went with it. The young woman did not need time to find out what might be the providential intimations for herself. Her heart was already in Oberlin's ownership; she arose, placed one hand before her eyes, and without a word spoken held out the other toward him. He clasped it in his own, and there is no record beyond this.

Oberlin never doubted after that that the intimation came from heaven; and assuredly it did. Their marriage followed soon, July 6, 1768, and Sophia, not Madeline, was the one who returned to live at Strasbourg. This happy matrimony was not in accord with the conventional mode formally arranged by parents, but it was a true love marriage. In Oberlin's records we see what an invaluable assistant she became to her husband in his indefatigable labors, tempering his zeal with her prudence and forwarding his plans by her wise cooperation. The qualities which she possessed he needed, and they made her influence of the greatest value. She fulfilled well her part in his endeavors for the betterment of these poor people, identifying herself with all that concerned her husband's vocation, cheerfully meeting his every consecration to the work of God with an equal one of her own. When the infant schools were started, she set the example for others by teaching. When the women of the parish were unwilling to learn to spin cotton in order to help the household earnings, which practice Oberlin introduced, his wife took the new industry in hand and led them on to the profits from it.

A quotation from a letter of Oberlin's well illustrates her spirit. An experimental school opened at Dessau, Germany which greatly interested Oberlin. He considered its methods the model for Germany. One of the professors there received a letter from Oberlin which said: "How I would like to spend weeks near you, to see and learn everything and return to the Ban-de-la-Roche to make this place in the mountains worthier by your knowledge! While reading your book with my wife we were saying, 'Why do we not have some of the money which is so useless in some hands.' We looked around to see if we could discover anything convertible to money. Suddenly my wife, beaming with joy, brought me a pair of earrings, asking to have them sent to aid your philanthropic institution. They cost her before marriage thirty florins. You can imagine how pleased I was. If the publication of my good little wife's name can influence others to follow her example, we cheerfully consent to it. Perhaps it may induce other people to make researches in their jewel boxes." Oberlin's life was both richer and stronger for this happy union, and his work from its beginning to its close bears the impress of her loving and beautiful character.

- Adapted from Augustus Field Beard's *The Story of John Frederick Oberlin*. Boston: Pilgrim Press, 1909.

Paton, John G. (1824-1907). Thrilling Escape Through Prayer.

Working as a soul-winner in his native Scotland, John Paton endured chamber pots thrown at him and other acts of opposition. Later as a missionary to the New Hebrides, he endured even more serious dangers.

MEN PASSED WITH FLAMING TORCHES; and first they set fire to the church all round, and then to a reed fence connecting the church and the house. In a few minutes the house, too, would be in flames, and armed savages waiting to kill us when we attempted an escape.

Taking my harmless revolver in the left hand and a little American tomahawk in the right, I pleaded with Mr. Mathieson to let me out and to lock the door on himself and wife. He very reluctantly did so, saying, "Stay here and let us die together. You will never return."

I said, "Be quick! Leave that to God. In a few minutes our house will be in flames, and then nothing can save us."

He let me out, and locked the door quickly from the inside; and while his wife and he prayed and watched for me from within, I ran to the burning reed fence, cut it from top to bottom, and tore it up and threw it back into the flames so that the fire could not be carried along it to our house. I saw on the ground shadows, as if something were falling around me, and started back. Seven or eight savages had surrounded me, and raised their great clubs in the air. I heard a shout, "Kill him! Kill him!"

One savage tried to seize hold of me, but, leaping from his clutch, I drew the revolver from my pocket and leveled it as if for use, my heart going up in prayer to my God. I said, "Dare to strike me and my Jehovah God will punish you. He protects us, and will punish you for burning His church, for hatred to His worship and people, and for all your bad conduct. We love you all; and it is only for doing you good that you want to kill us. But our God is here now to protect us and to punish you."

They yelled in rage, and urged each other to strike the first blow, but the Invisible One restrained them. I stood invulnerable beneath his invisible shield, and succeeded in rolling back the tide of flame from our dwelling.

At this dread moment occurred an incident, which my readers may explain as they like, but which I trace directly to the interposition of my God. A rushing and roaring sound came from the south, like the noise of a mighty engine or of muttering thunder. Every head was instinctively turned in that direction, and they knew from previous hard experience, that it was one of their awful tornadoes of wind and rain. Now, mark, the wind bore the flames away from our house; had it come in the opposite direction, no power on earth could have saved us from being all consumed! It made the work of destroying the church only that of a few minutes; but it brought with it a heavy murky cloud, which poured out a perfect torrent of tropical rain. Now, mark again, the flames of the burning church were thereby cut off from extending to and seizing upon the reeds and the bush; and, besides, it had become almost impossible now to set fire to our house...

The mighty roaring of the wind, the black cloud pouring down unceasing torrents, and the whole surroundings, awed those savages into silence. Some began to withdraw from the scene, all lowered their weapons of war, and several, terror-struck, exclaimed, "This is Jehovah's rain! Truly their Jehovah God is fighting for them and helping them. Let us away!"

A panic seized upon them; they threw away their remaining torches; in a few moments they had all disappeared in the bush; and I was left alone, praising God for all his marvelous works. "O, taste and see that God is good! Blessed is the man who trusts in Him!"

- Adapted from James Paton's *The Story of John G. Paton Told for Young Folks, or, thirty years among South Sea cannibals.* New York: A. L. Burt Company, 1892.

Peck, John Mason (1789-1858). One Hungry Preacher.

John Mason Peck became a prominent Baptist evangelist along the Mississippi River. Under his leadership, 32,000 souls were saved and 900 churches established. Although poorly educated, he saw the need of education and devoted much energy to rearing a Baptist college despite apathy and opposition. The result was Surtcliff College in Illinois.

ONCE, DURING FRONTIER DAYS in the United States, John Mason Peck set out at dawn to travel twenty miles to preach at a Missouri settlement at noon. Becoming lost, he had to retrace his steps and arrived around six o'clock at night. Because some of those waiting to hear him had long rides before them yet that night to return to their homes, he wasted no time getting to his sermon.

Afterward, his hostess asked him if he had taken dinner. The staunch preacher replied, "I propose first to eat breakfast. Then we will talk about dinner and supper."

- Adapted from internet sources and Reuben Herring's *The Baptist Almanac and Repository of Indispensable Knowledge.* Nashville, Tennessee: Broadman Press, 1976.

Penn, William (1644-1718). Brave Jurors Withstood Abuse to Win Civil Liberties; Fair Treatment of Indians;

William Penn, who converted to Quaker beliefs as a young man, is best-known as the founder of Pennsylvania and author of Fruits of Solitude.

Brave jurors. ON SUNDAY, AUGUST 14th, 1670, Friends [Quakers] found their meeting house in Gracechurch Street in the City of London guarded by soldiers. As a consequence, they met for worship in the street outside. William Penn was preaching when the police appeared, with warrants ready written by the lord mayor against him and William Mead, who was of the company. Penn gives an account of it in a letter to his father, written the next day from prison.

"Yesterday I was taken by a band of soldiers, with one Capt. Mead, a linen draper, and in the evening carried before the Mayor. He proceeded against me according to the ancient law; he told me I should have my hat pulled off, for all I was Admiral Penn's son. I told him that I desired to be in common with others, and sought no refuge from the common usage. He answered it had been no matter if you [Penn's father] had been a commander twenty years ago...He bade his clerk write me for Bridewell, and there would he see me whipped himself, for all I was Penn's son, that starved the seamen. Indeed, these words grieved me as well as that it manifested his great weakness and malice to the whole company, that were about one hundred people. I told him I could very well hear his severe expressions concerning myself, but was sorry to hear him speak those abuses of my father, that was not present, at which the assembly seemed to murmur."

Starling, the Lord Mayor, was a renegade Cromwellian, once a great persecutor of Royalists. The Friends were indicted at the Old Bailey on September 1. The charge was that the defendants, with other persons to the number of three hundred, did with force and arms unlawfully and tumultuously assemble and congregate themselves together to the disturbance of the peace—that William Penn, by agreement between him and William Mead, before made, and by abetment of the said William Mead, did take upon himself to preach and speak, by reason whereof a great concourse and tumult of people in the street did a long time remain and continue in contempt of the lord the king, and of his law; to the great disturbance of his peace, to the great terror of many of his lieges, and to the ill example of all others.

One can realize that the authorities could hardly afford to allow themselves to be baffled by this open-air demonstration of the Quakers whom they had turned out of doors. Thus does one bad course lead to another; and the path of compulsion descends rapidly to an intolerable place.

The trial occupied September 1st, 3rd, 4th and 5th. The justices were Sir Samuel Starling, the lord mayor, Sir John Howel, the recorder, five aldermen and three sheriffs.

At the beginning, the recorder refused the prisoners a copy of the lengthy indictment: which led Penn to demand that no undue advantage should be taken of this, and that he should have a fair hearing in defense. The two then pleaded not guilty.

The court adjourned, and the prisoners were made to stand aside while felons and murderers were tried—wearying and insulting them. After five hours, the court broke up without reaching their case. Two days later, on Saturday the third, they were again brought up, and the case began in earnest. The police had, with kindly intention, removed the prisoners' hats, which they had a conscientious objection to doing themselves [as showing undue respect to human authority], but the Bench were determined not to be denied their cunning device on this point, and ordered their hats to be put on again, and when they were brought up to the bar, they were fined forty marks apiece for contempt of court for having their hats on. Penn remarked that as the Bench was responsible for their hats being on, the Bench should be fined. The tone of the prisoners' minds comes out in William Mead's protest:

"I desire the Jury and all people to take notice of this injustice of the recorder, who spoke not to me to pull off my hat, and yet has he put a fine upon my head. O fear the Lord and dread His power, and yield to the guidance of His Holy Spirit, for He is not far from every one of you."

So far the Bench had not gained any moral weight, but had ensured that, whatever the verdict, the accused should go back to prison for not paying this fine.

The authorities seem to have known and feared Edward Bushel, one of the jurors, and pretended that he had not kissed the book; and so brought him up to swear again. He was thought to have a conscience against swearing twice. But the trick failed.

The police evidence was to the effect that they could not get near to William Penn because of the crowd, nor hear him because of the noise; but that William Mead had arranged that if William Penn was allowed peaceably to finish, he would give himself up at the close.

Then followed a long duel between the recorder and William Penn. The accused demanded by what law they were being tried, and the recorder refused information beyond saying that it was the Common Law, and abusing Penn as a saucy and impertinent fellow. Penn quoted Coke's *Institutes* and pleaded the privileges of Magna Carta. He managed to get out some forcible pleas in defense of liberty, and after many undignified attempts to silence him, they hauled him off to the "Bale Dock" at the far back of the court.

William Mead then stated in his defense that though once a Captain of the army he had now no freedom to use violence of any kind [as a pacifist Quaker], so could not be guilty of behaving *vi et armis*. He demanded an order of the law, and quoted Coke on the nature of a riot. Here the recorder interrupted him and thanked him for teaching him the law, scornfully pulling off his hat. On finding themselves no more a match for him than for Penn, and receiving from the prisoner a quantity of troublesome and impressive Latin, they sent him away also, to join his friend in the

Bale Dock. The recorder then charged the jury in the prisoners' absence; but he was interrupted by William Penn shouting from the distant Bale Dock, appealing against the charge being given in their absence, and quoting Coke again, on the right of prisoners to be heard. The only thing the recorder could do was to order the prisoners into "the hole," a stinking place in Newgate, close by, where they were safely out of hearing. Penn describes this foul place as not fit for pigs. The jury debated an hour and a half. Then eight walked in and agreed to convict. The four dissentients were ordered down also, among them Edward Bushel, the hero of this story.

The recorder threatened him. "I shall set a mark upon you, sir." Other aldermen and the lord mayor abused him, and sent the jury back. After a considerable time they returned unanimous. "William Penn is guilty of speaking in Gracechurch Street."

This would never do. But not another word would the jury consent to say. They were sent back for half an hour, but returned with a similar verdict in writing. The court fell upon Bushel and Thomas Vere, the foreman, and threatened to lock the jury up without meat, drink, fire or tobacco, till they revised their verdict. Penn vigorously interfered in defense of his jury.

"The agreement of twelve men is a verdict in law, and such a one being given by the jury, I require the clerk of the court to record it, as he will answer it at his peril and if the jury bring in another verdict contrary to this, I affirm they are perjured men in law. (And looking upon the jury said) "You are Englishmen, mind your privilege, don't give away your rights."

"We won't ever do that," responded the jurymen.

One juryman pleaded illness, but the court refused to release him. "Starve and hold your principles." They were kept all night without food or drink, or any other necessity. At seven the next day, Sunday, the court met again, but the jury's verdict was unchanged.

The court fell upon Bushel. "That conscience of yours would cut my throat," remarked the lord mayor.

"No, my lord, it never shall," replied the juror.

"But I will cut yours as soon as I can," replied the lord mayor. The recorder, not to be outdone in throwing away his dignity added, "He has inspired the jury; he has the spirit of divination: methinks I feel him. I will have a positive verdict, or you shall starve for it."

Penn now intervened on behalf of Mead, who ought to be liberated on the verdict: and as the charge was for conspiracy, he should be freed, too, as one man cannot conspire alone. But the recorder declared that Not Guilty was no verdict. He threatened to pursue Bushel with future vengeance, and the lord mayor said he would slit his [Bushel's] nose. Penn intervened with a defense of the rights of juries, and the lord mayor ordered him to be fettered and fastened to the ground. The recorder longed audibly for the Inquisition in England, and promised a new act of complete outlawry for Nonconformists in the next session of Parliament. He then ordered the clerk to draw up another verdict for the jury to adopt; but he said he did not know how. The recorder threatened to starve the jury, and cart them round the city. They were sent upstairs again with a threat of force, and kept again without food, drink, or sanitary accommodation all night. At seven in the morning of Monday, the court met again; and received a direct verdict of

"Not Guilty" from the indomitable jury, now pale and weak. Each juryman was then compelled to give the verdict separately and did so. Each said, "Not Guilty;" the people in the court were evidently delighted. Penn says they made a sort of hymn. Clearly bullying would not overcome this jury. The court then dared to fine them forty marks each, and send them to prison till it was paid. Penn and Mead accompanied them to Newgate for not paying their fines for contempt of court about the hats: not however without a final appeal from William Penn to the fundamental liberties of Englishmen from the inquisition so dear to the recorder's heart.

For two days and nights this brave jury endured the cruelty of these miserable Restoration magistrates. Some were in high fever, some wandered in their minds, from overstrain, lack of sleep and raging thirst. Their room had become foul. They supported one another in the dark hours of misery, weakness strengthening weakness, with the strength of an overcoming spirit. They did much to save trial by jury for the Englishmen that have followed them. Their case became the classic one on the independence of juries.

Penn wrote to his father that the jury were determined to lie in prison till they could be legally released without paying their fine, and that, by advice of counsel, they demanded their liberty every six hours. They were released after a few days by the Court of Common Pleas, their commitment being pronounced illegal. Thus the final victory was won. Twelve judges, after an elaborate trial and notable speeches of counsel, decided unanimously that a jury alone is the judge of the facts, and that "the court may try to open they eyes of the jurors, but not to lead them by the nose." To

Bushel and his companions, Englishmen owe one of the strongholds of their freedom from bureaucratic tyranny.

- Adapted from John W. Graham's *William Penn; founder of Pennsylvania*. London: Headley Bros. Publishers, Ltd., 1916.

Fair treatment of Indians. That Penn treated the Indians as neighbors and brothers; that he paid them fairly for every acre of their land; that the promises which he made were ever after unfailingly kept is perhaps his best warrant of abiding fame. Like his constitutional establishment of civil and religious liberty, it was a direct result of his Quaker principles. It was a manifestation of that righteousness which he was continually preaching and practicing.

The kindness and courtly generosity which Penn showed in his bargains with the Indians is happily illustrated in one of his purchases of land. The land was to extend "as far back as a man can walk in three days." William walked out a day and a half, reasoning that it would take a day and a half to walk back, bringing the total to three days. He took several chiefs with him, "Leisurely, after the Indian manner, sitting down sometimes to smoke their pipes, to eat biscuit and cheese, and drink a bottle of wine." Thus they covered less than thirty miles.

By contrast, in 1733 when another governor made a similar deal, he employed the fastest walker he could find, who by the middle of the third day had covered 86 miles.

- Adapted from George Hodges. *William Penn*. Boston and New York: Houghton Mifflin Co., 1901.

Perronet, Edward (1726-1792). The Greatest Sermon Ever Preached.

Edward Perronet, author of the beloved hymn "All Hail the Power of Jesus' Name," was a preacher associated with the Wesleys and more than once roughed up for preaching.

PERRONET WAS UNEASY about preaching in front of the famous John Wesley. After several pleas which he turned down, Wesley saw he could not persuade him, and put the younger man on the spot one day by announcing, "Brother Perronet will speak." With quick wit, Perronet more than matched Wesley's ruse. He entered the pulpit, declaring he would deliver the greatest sermon ever preached, and proceeded to read Christ's "Sermon on the Mount," after which he promptly sat down.

- This story is widely circulated and appears on many web sites.

Peters, Hugh (1599-1660). Free Gospel Passage; Wounded Friend.

Hugh Peters was a preacher who fled England after falling afoul of Archbishop Laud. Sent by American colonists to conduct some business for them, he became an army chaplain in the English Civil War and served for a time as secretary to Oliver Cromwell. Charles II had him executed after the Restoration, and many lies were circulated to make him appear a buffoon. He did have a strong wit as these anecdotes shows.

Gospel passage. DISCOURSING OF THE ADVANTAGE Christians have above heathen, and showing that the heathen are guided by a natural instinct, but we have the word preached to us, Peters said, "The Gospel has a very free passage among us—for I am confident it no sooner enters in at one ear, but it is out at the other."

Wounded friend. MR. PETERS ENCOUNTERED a friend of his, deeply cut in the head, having gotten into a foolish fight. He began to scold him for his folly, but, checked himself, saying, "It is too late now to give you counsel; come along with me to a surgeon, and I'll see your wound dressed." The surgeon washed away the blood, and searched for his brains, to see if they were hurt. At which Mr. Peters cried out, "What a madman you are to look for any such thing; if he had possessed any brains he would never have ventured into so foolish a contest."

- Both anecdotes are adapted from Charles Spurgeon's *Eccentric Preachers*. London: Passmore and Alabaster, 1879.

Phillips, Wendell (1811-1884). Defines Heroism.

Wendell was a New Yorker who became a champion against slavery partly from conscience and partly through the influence of the woman who became his wife. His stand made him controversial and hated. He was one of the great speakers of his day, noted for the conversational tone of his speeches.

AN AUTOGRAPH HUNTER accosted Phillips one day. The old man held his visitor far toward night, showing him relics of the abolitionists and memorials of his own labors. He was about to bid the young man good evening when the latter, half patronizingly said, "Mr. Phillips, I think if I had lived in your time, I would have been heroic, too."

Phillips as he stood in the doorway pointed to the open places of iniquity near his dwelling place, and said, "Young man, you are living in my time, and in God's time. Did you hear Francis Willard last night?" [Willard was a prominent temperance advocate.] "Be assured, no man would have been heroic then who is not heroic now. Good night."

- Adapted from Anna A. Gordon. *The Beautiful Life of Frances E. Willard*. Chicago, Illinois: Women's Temperance Publishing Association, 1898.

Pike, Kenneth (1912-2000). Carrying His Three Stones.

Ken Pike was a gifted linguist and Bible translator. At one time, he was nominated for a Nobel Prize.

PIKE HAD MADE A POINT of respecting the elders of San Miguel and he called himself a resident of the town, in his effort to connect with its people. Instead of paying taxes, the locals performed certain tasks, such as carrying stones for the construction of a public building. Outsiders were automatically excluded. But Ken did not want to be an outsider.

One day he astonished the mayor and the other men by appearing with a large rock tied to his back and dropped it on a pile intended for a public project. The mayor solemnly accepted it and told him he needed two more. (Each man's quota was three.)

At some risk to his body (he had broken his leg some time before and it was still weak), Ken brought in the other two rocks. After that, the community showed its acceptance by saying, "He carried his three rocks."

- Adapted from Eunice Pike's *Ken Pike, Scholar and Christian*. Dallas, Texas. Summer Institute of Linguistics, 1981.

Pryor, Mary Bray (1737-1815). A Witty Retort.

Not a name to find its way into Christian histories, Mary Pryor was nonetheless typical of many godly Quakers and respected in her own generation on both sides of the Atlantic. This brief anecdote by a great-granddaughter gives an indication why.

SHE AGAIN SHOWED HER DECISION of character, when, if report be true, she was asked by a rich merchant (the founder of the Hope family) to become his second wife, and refused to the chagrin of her old nurse, who is said to have remarked, "You might have eaten gold," receiving from her young mistress the smart and wise reply, "But I could not have digested it."

- Mary Pryor Hack. *Mary Pryor; a life story of a hundred years ago.* Philadelphia: H. Longstreth, 1888.

Radstock, Lord (1833-1913). The Lord Disposes; A Keen Sense of Humor.

Lord Radstock had been a Christian for years but done nothing for Jesus. One day he was challenged to read to a man in a hospital. The man was converted. Elated, Radstock ever afterward devoted himself to winning souls, dressing plainly, going hungry and giving up shooting so that he might tell others about Christ.

The Lord arranges what man cannot. LORD RADSTOCK'S LIFE was one of prayer without ceasing. A friend tells me of an incident common enough in the lives of those who live close to God, but worth recording. He was on his way to India, the vessel was very full, and it  was impossible to secure a cabin to himself. This was essential, for on board ship spiritual conversation and prayer is often impossible otherwise. In vain the authorities tried to arrange it. Lord Radstock's resource was prayer. The bell sounded, and the vessel was about to leave, names were called out, each passenger responding, but in vain the name of Mr. S. was called. Mr. S. was to have occupied the vacant berth in Lord Radstock's cabin. The vessel started without the missing passenger, and God's servant was thus given the opportunity he needed.

A keen sense of humor. Lord Radstock had a keen sense of humor. Meeting an influential member of the Evangelical Alliance, Lord Radstock quoted a remarkable statement without mentioning by whom it was made, adding, "Would not the man who spoke this be worthy of the Evangelical Alliance?"

"Indeed he would," responded his friend enthusiastically. "Do let us get him to join us!"

"He is the Pope!" said Lord Radstock, thoroughly enjoying the joke.

- Both episodes are adapted from Mrs. Edward Trotter's *Lord Radstock; an Interpretation and a Record*. London: Hodder & Stoughton, ca. 1914.

Radzivil, Nicolas (1515-1565). The Making of a Reformer.

Nicolas "the Black" was the leader of the Protestant faction in Lithuania, and his nation's most important official, the Palatine of Vilna, to whom John Calvin dedicated the second edition of the second volume of his commentary on the Acts of the Apostles.

WHEN THE REFORMATION spread in Lithuania, Prince Radzivil was at first no supporter, but went in person to pay the pope all possible honors. His Holiness on this occasion presented him with a precious box of relics.

The prince having returned home, some monks entreated permission to try the effects of these relics on a demoniac, who had hitherto resisted every kind of exorcism. The box of bones was brought into the church with solemn pomp, and deposited on the altar, accompanied by an innumerable crowd. After the usual conjurations, which were unsuccessful, they applied the relics. The demoniac instantly recovered. The people called out "a miracle!" and the prince, lifting his hands and eyes to heaven, felt his faith confirmed. In this transport of pious joy, he observed that a young gentleman, who was keeper of this treasure of relics, smiled, and by his motions ridiculed the miracle. The prince indignantly took the young keeper of the relics to task, who, on promise of pardon, gave the following secret intelligence concerning them. In traveling from Rome he had lost the box of relics; and not daring to mention it, he had procured a similar one, which he had filled with the small bones of dogs and cats, and other trifles similar to what were lost. He hoped he might be forgiven for smiling, when he found that such a collection of rubbish was idolized with such pomp, and had even the virtue of expelling demons. It was by the assistance of this box that the prince discovered the gross impositions of the monks and the demoniacs, and Radzivil afterwards became a zealous Protestant.

- Adapted from Isaac D'Israeli's *Curiosities of Literature.* London: Frederick and Warne, 1881.

Ramabai, Pandita (1858-1922). Her Prayer Life.

Pandita Ramabai was reared a Hindu and trained in Hindu languages and literature by a father who rejected the notion that women should not learn. Consequently, she became the first notable female Hindu scholar, whose example helped break the chains of Indian women. Her own chains fell off when she became a Christian. She then opened a major Christian work to rescue, educate, and train widows in India.

IT HAD LONG BEEN HER CUSTOM to rise a great while before day and busy herself in her own room, before the secular labors of the day commenced, with the labor of prayer and intercession. Her diary of the routine of daily duty begins with the words, "The big church bell rang at 4 a.m. to rouse everybody from sleep. I was up." Four a.m. seems early enough to arouse anyone, but an earlier call still had already aroused her. On urgent occasions she also fasted. In the case of one with so vivid a faith in God, and burdened at the same time by so heavy and so constant a responsibility, it was the most natural thing in the world to pray and scarcely less so at times to fast.

This practical woman watched for the results from her prayers, and, when they came, her confidence in Him to whom she committed all her troubles was strengthened. There are many stories of the answers she received, but Manoramabai tells one which may serve as a sample. One of the grass huts in which in 1901, many of the rescued women were housed, caught fire. The wind was from the east and carrying the flames swiftly towards the school buildings. The danger was extreme. "Mother was of course praying all the time that God would help us in some way or other. The men were working as hard as possible, but they, too, were beginning to despair when, suddenly, in a most marvelous manner, the direction of the wind changed and it began blowing from the east, thus causing the fire to recede."

- Nicol MacNicol. *Pandita Ramabai.* Calcutta: Association Press, 1926.

Randal, Elder Benjamin (1749 -1808). Baptizes Despite Murder Attempt.

Randal found fault with George Whitefield when he heard him preach, but soon afterward Whitefield died and this shook Randal, who realized that Whitefield had been a genuine man of God. He sought salvation and found it. He joined a group of Baptists, but they cast him off because he did not hold their Calvinism. Randal then founded the Free Will Baptists, and was a mighty laborer for souls, traveling thousands of miles a year through New England to preach the Gospel and plant churches despite a sometimes furious opposition.

ONE DAY AS HE WAS ABOUT TO ADMINISTER BAPTISM to a number of candidates, he proceeded to a small millpond, which was convenient. The man who owned the pond, feeling great opposition to Randal, resolved to deprive him of the privilege of baptizing in it. He ran immediately to his mill, and hoisted both gates to draw off the water, and so disappoint him. Randal observing that the water was fast falling, without knowing the intention of the man, said, "Our heavenly Father has given us water to baptize in, and we must improve it while we have it;" and began to baptize. Finding himself disappointed, the man ran with great violence to the bridge, and taking up a club in his hand, threw it at Randal as he was baptizing; but someone caught his arm, and stopped its force, so that it fell short and dropped into the water. The man hurled several more clubs but bystanders checked their force in the same way. Randal saw the clubs falling into the water, but being solemnly engaged, did not ask why until all the candidates were baptized; then coming up out of the water, and seeing a tumult among the people on the bridge, he inquired the cause of it. He was told that there was a man on the bridge, who had been trying to kill him while he had been baptizing. "Where is the dear soul," said Randal, "Let me go and speak to him."

Pushing through the crowd, he came to the man, and began to address him in the most loving manner. But the man scowled, drew back his arm, and directed his fist at Randal's face. No doubt the blow would have proved painful, but some friendly persons who were standing by, jerked Randal out of the man's reach. "Why did you not let him strike me?" said Randal, "it might have been the means of the conversion of his dear soul." He never appeared to value what he suffered, if he could but see souls converted. This same year, the work of the Lord spread in a very rapid manner through the country round about, and many were converted.

- Adapted from John Buzzell. *The Life of Elder Benjamin Randal.* Limerick, Maine: Hobbs, Woodman & Co., 1827.

Raper, William H. (1793-1852). Deliverance by Prayer.

William H. Raper was something of a young hero in the War of 1812, showing great presence of mind when, with just five soldiers, he quelled a mutiny of 100 prisoners of war. He was a member of the Methodist's Western Conference for 33 years.

AS WILLIAM RAPER was crossing a stream, his horse became entangled while swimming and sank, throwing him off. It was a cold morning, a little before sunrise; and being encumbered with heavy clothing, he found it difficult to swim, but with great effort he succeeded in catching hold of the limb of a tree, which was hanging over the stream, where he was able to rest and hold his head above the water.

While suspended in the stream, the thought rushed upon him, "My mother is praying for me, and I shall be saved." After resting a moment or two, he made another effort and got ashore. His horse also made a safe landing, having the saddle bags all safe. Raper's clothes and books were drenched, however, and he himself much chilled by the early bath.

Meanwhile, while he was battling with the stream, his mother, some eighty or a hundred miles distant, suddenly awoke with a fright, and the thought rushed upon her, "William is in great danger." She sprang from her bed, and falling upon her knees, prayed for some time in intense supplication for his safety, after which she received a sweet assurance that all was well. When they met and related the facts, and compared the times, they precisely agreed.

- Adapted from Finley's *Sketches of Western Methodism* as quoted by George Coles in *Heroines of Methodism*. New York: Carlton & Lanahan, 1869.

Roberts, Benjamin Titus (1823-1893). Taking the Side of the Underdog.

Benjamin Roberts ran afoul of his Methodist denomination for pointing out some dangerous trends, and was stripped of his ordination; so he founded the Free Methodist Church in association with J. W. Redfield and others. He was its first General Superintendent (Bishop). The Methodists later acknowledged they had wronged him. As a young man, Roberts championed the abolition of slavery; after emancipation, he took the side of newly-liberated blacks.

ONCE WHEN ROBERTS WAS TRAVELING on train a man remonstrated with the conductor for not ordering a decently dress, well-behaved company of young black people into the second-class car. The conductor told him that they had first-class tickets, but in spite of this the objector grew very vehement in his protestations against being obliged to ride with "niggers" (as he called them). Upon this, Roberts interposed in their behalf and urged their cause convincingly. They remained in first class.

Before they left the car, they gathered about him and their spokesman thanked him in cultivated language. Then, still gathered around him, they sang a most beautiful song. The group, it turned out, was one of the first troupes of Jubilee Singers from Fiske University, whose spirituals so stirred the nation to an appreciation of what the black man could do when they had the school-master instead of the overseer for their guide.

- Adapted from Benson Howard Roberts' *Benjamin Titus Roberts, a Biography*. North Chili, New York: "The Earnest Christian" Offices, 1900; p. 565.

Roberts, Robert R. (1778-1843). A Brush with Drowning; Traveling Incognito.

Robert Richford Roberts risked his life as a Methodist circuit rider and became the first married bishop of the Methodist church. His biographer recounts several instances in which he was in peril and also notes that he did not like to say who he was unless pressed, even if it meant he had to go hungry.

Close to drowning. IN 1828, when Bishop Roberts was traveling from Lawrenceport to Cincinnati by way of Aurora and Lawrenceburg, he spent a night with a pastor a few miles below the junction of the Whitewater and Miami Rivers. Both streams were in Spring flood. The regular ferry was not running on account of the high water, but the pastor, J. H. Brower, thought he could get the bishop over since Roberts was anxious to keep an engagement in Cincinnati.

The Bishop, a mail-carrier, two other men and Brower embarked. The current was rapid, and the lower oar snapped in two, leaving all at the mercy of the raging stream. They floated rapidly toward a mass of driftwood. Had they struck it, they would have been instantly dashed in pieces. The only alternative was to steer the boat between a number of large trees, partly under water. However, the gunwale of the boat struck a tree, and the force of the current against the upper side pressed it down, so that the water poured over it in mass, and almost filled it in a moment. At this desperate juncture, Brower yelled to the Bishop to drive his horse overboard, which he promptly did, while a blow from the broken oar drove the mail-carrier's horse after him. By this expedient the boat was lightened enough that, by Herculean exertion, they managed to push off from the tree, and reach the shore, full of water. Immediately the vessel sank.

The horses survived but the mail bags were lost. During the crisis the Bishop maintained perfect calmness and self-command. Upon reaching the shore, he spread his handkerchief on the wet and muddy ground, and kneeling down, was quiet for several minutes before breaking out in the language of the 46th Psalm, "God is our refuge and strength; a very present help in trouble. Therefore will we not fear, though the earth be removed, and though the mountains be carried into the midst of the sea; though the waters thereof roar and be troubled." And then he poured out a burst of gratitude for the sustaining and preserving mercies of God upon which he relied.

Incognito embarrassment. ONCE THE BISHOP put up at a tavern. The landlord, who did not know him, was going to a class meeting (Bible study and prayer) and excused himself. "If you want to go to bed before we return," he said, handing him a candle, "you may take a bed in the next room."

The bishop asked if he might go to the class meeting instead, if it was not intruding. "No intrusion at all," replied the landlord. "We allow serious persons to attend class meeting a few times without becoming members, if they wish."

The class leader, a young man with more zeal than experience, inquired of the bishop, "Well, stranger, have you any desire to serve the Lord and to get to heaven?"

"I have such a desire," replied the bishop.

"How long have you had this desire?"

"I cannot say precisely how long now, but for many years."

"Well, do you think, old gentleman, that you know anything about the enjoyment of experimental religion?"

"Yes, brother," answered the bishop, "I trust I do know, and have known a long time what experimental religion is; though I acknowledge I have not been as faithful as I should have been; and, consequently, have not made that progress in religion which it was my privilege to have made. Still I have a good hope in the mercy of God, through Christ, that I shall be saved in heaven at last."

The class leader gave him counsel, as was the custom, and closed the meeting, and the landlord walked back to the tavern with Roberts. After they had been seated a short time, the landlord brought in a table, with a Bible and a hymnbook. He looked at the Bible and then at the bishop. After a few side glances, he rose, and started toward the table; then stopped, cleared his throat, and went to the door and spit; then turned again toward the table; but finally stopped, and said, "Old gentleman, you appear to be a man who knows something of religion. It is our custom to have family worship. Perhaps you would be willing to read and pray with us?"

"I have no objection, brother, if you wish it," answered Roberts, and then proceeded to read from the Bible and to sing and pray.

The landlord then took a candle, showed him his room; started out, got to the door, stopped, turned round, hesitated, and finally asked his name, "If it would be no offense."

"No offense at all, brother: my name is Robert R. Roberts."

When he told this anecdote, Roberts added: "And they paid me well for telling my name; for they detained me two days, and made me preach several times." He would not say how the young class leader looked at the close of the first sermon.

- Adapted from Worth Marion Tippy's *Frontier Bishop, The Life and Times Of Robert Richford Roberts*. New York: Abingdon Press, 1867, 1958 (Public Domain).

Robinson, Reuben "Bud" (1860-1942). Only One Conscience.

When Bud Robinson got saved as a young man, he did not know how to read or write. He stammered horribly, and suffered epilepsy and bleeding from the lungs. However, determined to win souls, he preached in spite of all impediments. After struggling for years against personal sins such as a hot temper, he experienced a transformation which led him to believe in sanctification as a second work of grace. He became a leader and editor in the Nazarene church.

THE ELDER WHO HAD DIRECT AUTHORITY over Bud was opposed to his teaching on holiness and confronted him at quarterly conference. "You will give up your conscience on the subject of sanctification as a second work of grace, or you will give up the Methodist Church."

With his usual grit Bud answered, "I have but one conscience, and, as there are many churches, I will keep my conscience."

Because of this answer, he was forced out of the Southern Methodist conference.

In his struggle for holiness, the colorful preacher said he prayed, "O Lord, give me a backbone as big as a saw log and ribs like the sleepers under the church floor; put iron shoes on me and galvanized breeches and hang a wagonload of determination up in the gable end of my soul, and help me to sign a contract to fight the devil as long as I have a vision, and bite him as long as I have a tooth, and then gum him until I die."

- Retold from Basil Miller's *Bud Robinson, Miracle of Grace.* Kansas City, Missouri: Beacon Hill, 1947.

Rohner, Fräulein Beatrice (Twentieth Century). Eyewitness to the Armenian Massacre.

Under cover of World War I, the Turks massacred or drove into exile virtually their entire Christian population, one and a half million Armenians. For the most part the men were massacred outright while the women and children were killed more slowly by marching them through deserts until they dropped of exhaustion. Gendarmes were told they could take the prettiest girls for themselves and the rape of the poor creatures was carried out openly in the streets. Many eyewitness accounts have come to us, some too horrifying to be included in this book. This record is by a Swiss missionary.

FOR THESE MOUNTAINEERS the desert climate is terrible. On the next day I reached a large Armenian camp of goat-skin tents, but most of the unfortunate people were sleeping out in the sun on the burning sands. The Turks had given them a day's rest on account of the large number of sick. It was evident from their clothing that these people had been well-to-do; they were natives of Geben, another village near Zeitoun, and were led by their religious head. It was a daily occurrence for five or six of the children of these people to die by the wayside. They were just burying a young woman, the mother of a little girl nine years of age, and they besought me to take this little girl with me.

Those who have no experience of the desert cannot picture to themselves the sufferings entailed by such a journey—a hilly desert without shade marching over rough and rugged rocks and unable to satisfy one's scorching thirst from the muddy waters of the Euphrates, which winds its course along in close proximity.

On the next day I met another camp of these Zeitoun Armenians. There were the same indescribable sufferings, the same accounts of misery—"Why do they not kill us once for all?" asked they. "For days we have no water to drink, and our children are crying for water. At night the Arabs attack us; they steal our bedding, our clothes that we have been able to get together; they carry away by force our girls and outrage our women. If any of us are unable to walk, the convoy of gendarmes beat us. Some of our women threw themselves down from the rocks into the Euphrates in order to save their honor—some of these with infants in their arms."

- Arnold J. Toynbee *Armenian Atrocities; the murder of a nation.* London: Hodder and Stoughton, 1915.

Rutherford, Samuel (ca. 1600-1661). Higher Summons.

Samuel Rutherford was a Scottish Presbyterian preacher and theologian, and the author of Lex Rex, *a treatise that called for separation of governmental powers, a constitution, and limited government. He greatly influenced John Locke. His letters show much spiritual depth.*

STRIPPED OF ALL POSTS and offices in the University and in prison, Rutherford was summoned to appear before Parliament on a charge of high treason. When the messengers arrived with their summons, the dying old man responded, "Tell them that I have got a summons already from a superior Judge and Judicatory, and I find it necessary to answer my first summons, and before your day arrives, I will be where few kings and great folks come."

- Adapted from Walter Baxendale's *Dictionary of Anecdote, Incident, Illustrative Fact.* New York: Thomas Whittaker, 1889.

Ryan, Patrick John (1831-1911). Railroad Counsel.

Patrick John Ryan was the second Archbishop of Philadelphia.

ARCHBISHOP RYAN once attended a dinner given him by the citizens of Philadelphia, and a brilliant company of men were present. Among others were the president of the Pennsylvania Railroad; ex-Attorney-General MacVeagh, counsel for the road; and other prominent railroad men.

MacVeagh, in talking to the guest of the evening, said: "Your Grace, among others you see here a great many railroad men. There is a peculiarity of railroad men that even on social occasions you will find that they always take their lawyer with them. That is why I am here. They never go anywhere without their counsel. Now they have nearly everything that men want, but I have a suggestion to make to you for an exchange with us. We can give free passes on all the railroads of the country. Now if you would only give us—say a free pass to Paradise by way of exchange."

"Ah, no," said His Grace, with a merry twinkle in his eye, "that would never do. I would not like to separate them from their counsel."

- James Gilchris Lawson. *The world's Best Humorous Anecdotes; wit and repartee selected from many sources* and arranged topically by J. Gilchrist Lawson. New York, George H. Doran Co., 1923.

Sang, Mansur (Twentieth Century). Priceless.

Mansur Sang, a Muslim Dervish became a Christian. Before his conversion, he had begged for a living. Afterward, he saw that as a Christian he should make his own way. He did so by pulling teeth, which was done in public. When a crowd gathered to observe, he would whip out his Bible and preach.

ARRESTED IN IRAN, he was brought to a station where the chief of police was a Baha'i. The chief flipped through some tracts confiscated from Mansur and asked how much he sold them for. Mansur replied that he gave them free to anyone was truly interested in reading them. "This shows that your religion isn't worth anything," said the chief. "You have to give your literature away." He pointed to a shelf of Baha'i books and said he had paid a great sum for them.

Mansur then pointed to the electric lights in the office and asked if the electricity had to be paid for. He was told yes. Mansur then pointed to the sun and asked if its light had to be paid for.

Naturally he was told no.

Mansur then replied, "Your books, like these electric light fixtures, are man-made and give a little light, but you have to pay for them. This Scripture is the Word of God and has the light of the sun. And just the way the sunshine is free, so this is free to those who will receive it."

- Retold from J. Christy Wilson Jr.'s *More to Be Desired than Gold*. South Hamilton, Massachusetts: Gordon-Conwell Seminary, 1992.

Sankey, Ira D. (1840-1908). Wet Witness; Fire Song.

Sankey was for many years the song evangelist for Dwight L. Moody.

Wet witnesses. DURING ALL OUR CAMPAIGNS abroad it was Moody's and my custom to rest on Saturdays, and to make excursions into the country on that day, whenever it was convenient. While at Sutherland, England, one Saturday, we took a cab and drove a few miles northward along the seashore. Coming to an almost perpendicular cliff rising hundreds of feet above the level of the sea, we descended by a stairway to the beach below. For a while we enjoyed ourselves by walking along the shore, examining the beautiful shells left exposed by the tide, which had gone out before we arrived.

Our attention was soon arrested by someone shouting from the top of the cliff. We saw a man wildly beckoning to us to return. On looking around we discovered that the tide had risen and had filled the deep channel between us and the stairway. It was clear that we had no time to lose. Mr. Moody suggested that I should plunge in and lead the way to the cliff as quickly as possible, and while I did so he stood looking on, convulsed with laughter at my frantic strides through the water over the slippery stones. But I reached a place of safety, and it was my opportunity to enjoy a sight not soon to be forgotten, as my friend slowly and with considerable difficulty waded through the constantly rising water to the place where I stood.

We were to hold a Bible reading that afternoon at three o'clock. Not having time to go to our lodgings for a change of clothing, we at once proceeded to the place of meeting, and we held the service in our wet clothes and shoes.

A song in fire. SANKEY WAS CAUGHT in the terrible Chicago fire, but managed to escape to Lake Michigan where he found a small boat and tied it up to some timbers erected for a new breakwater. On these he perched for most of the night, watching as the flames consumed the city. From time to time he heard great explosions, as General Sheridan's men blew up houses in the path of the conflagration. As the fire died down, he stepped back into the boat, but the rope snapped, and he was nearly swept out by currents, but he soon got the boat under control and made landfall.

While on the lake he sang:

Dark is the night, and cold the wind is blowing,
Nearer and nearer comes the breakers' roar;
Where shall I go, or whither fly for refuge?
Hide me, my Father, till the storm is o'er.

- Both stories are from Ira D. Sankey's *My Life and the Story of the Gospel Hymns*. Philadelphia: Sunday School Times, 1907.

Sayers, Dorothy (1893-1957). Shredded Contract.

> *Dorothy Sayers was a witty Christian scholar and the author of the popular Lord Peter Wimsey mysteries, as well as essays defending the Christian faith, a verse translation of Dante, and several plays, including* The Man Born to Be King, *a cycle which retold the life of Christ for radio during World War II.*

EARLY IN 1941, a producer's assistant sent back one of Dorothy's plays from the cycle *The Man Born to Be King* with suggestions for "improvements." Dorothy, a successful author and careful craftsman, did not care to have others tell her how to write. Infuriated, she tore her contract to shreds and mailed the pieces to the B.B.C. The B.B.C. backed down.

* Retold from Alzina Stone Dale's *Maker and Craftsman; the story of Dorothy L. Sayers.* Grand Rapids: Eerdman's, 1978.

Scudder, Ida (1870-1960). Earthly Mansion.

Ida Scudder was an extraordinary medical missionary to India, and founder of Vellore hospital and medical school.

IDA SCUDDER GAVE UP MANY DREAMS to work as a doctor in India. For years she imagined building a summer home on a particularly beautiful hill in Kodaikanal. She promised herself if the opportunity ever came, she would try to acquire the hill property, which was especially desirable for its view. In 1922, just before she was committed to return to the U.S. on furlough, she learned that eight desirable acres were soon to go on the market. She could not change her plans, so waited as long as she could for the auction to be announced. Her furlough took her away first, so she commissioned her brother Walter to act in her behalf. The sale still was not announced. Commitments required Walter to leave. Before he did so, he recruited a local missionary to bid in Ida's behalf. Four months later, the date of sale was finally posted: 8 a.m. September 15th.

No one appeared except the land agent and Ida's representative. "It is eight o'clock," said he.

"But no one is here," protested the land agent.

"I'm here and I wish to place a bid." Under the posted terms the land agent had to accept the offer, which was just over the minimum required by the terms of sale—about one hundred American dollars, equivalent to perhaps $5,000 in 2006. Other bidders appeared later that day with far larger sums, but were told they were too late.

On the site, Ida erected Hill Top, her pleasant retirement home. Spacious and beautiful, it was created with every bit of the zest that characterized all her endeavors; friends teased her she was trying to have her heavenly mansion on earth.

- Retold from the account in Dorothy Clarke Wilson's *Dr. Ida; the story of Dr. Ida Scudder of Vellore.* New York: McGraw-Hill Book Co., 1959.

Selwyn, George (1809-1878). Humble Enough for a Pigsty.

George Selwyn was the first bishop of New Zealand. During the long war between the Maori and the Colonists, he kept the confidence of both sides. At his insistence the New Zealand church allowed equal participation for Maori Christians from its start.

SELWYN CARED DEEPLY for the Maori, so much so that he learned their language, risked his life, and humbled himself to win them for Christ. When the Maori were fighting the British in an effort to retain their land, Selwyn arranged a conference with them. The Maori, assuming that he would side with the British soldiers, determined to humiliate him. When he arrived that evening, they barred him from their hall, but said he could spend the night in a pigsty.

Selwyn cheerfully agreed. Driving out the pigs, he gathered ferns for bedding and slept in the pen. This act of humility deeply impressed the Maori. Not only did they agree to talks, but said, "You cannot degrade the dignity of this man."

- Retold from F. W. Boreham's *Mountains in the Mist*. Grand Rapids: Kregel, 1995 and his Cliffs of Opal. London: Epworth, 1948.

Seville Council (633). Hymns Are Controversial.

IN 633, Spaniards held a council in Seville at which they debated the use of hymns. Was it right to use mere, man-made words in worship? At stake were the use of texts composed by Ambrose and Hilary, of which this is a fair representation:

> O Trinity of blessed light,
> O Unity of princely might,
> The fiery sun now goes his way,
> Shed You within our hearts a ray.
> To You our morning song of praise,
> To You our evening prayer we raise;
> O grant us with Your saints on high
> To praise You through eternity...

Led by Isidore of Seville, the council determined that hymn use was acceptable.

- Compiled from a number of sources, including *The Catholic Encyclopedia*.

Sidney, Sir Philip (1554-1586). A Gallant Sacrifice.

Sidney was a gallant at the court of Elizabeth and a famous poet, whose works appear in English anthologies. He also wrote a spirited defense of poetry.

AT THE BATTLE of Zutphen, in the Netherlands, after having two horses killed under him, Sir Philip Sidney received a wound while in the act of mounting a third, and was carried bleeding, faint, and thirsty to the camp. A small quantity of water was brought to allay his thirst; but as he was raising it to his lips, he observed a poor wounded soldier, who was carried past at the moment, look at the cup with wistful eyes. The generous Sidney instantly withdrew it untasted from his mouth, and gave it to the soldier, saying, "Your necessity is yet greater than mine." He died of his wound, aged only thirty-three; but his kindness to the poor soldier has caused his name to be remembered ever since with admiration, and it will probably never be forgotten while humane and generous actions are appreciated among men.

- Adapted from *The Book of Three Hundred Anecdotes Historical, Literary, and Humorous—A New Selection.* London and New York: Burns & Oates, n.d.

Simeon, Charles (1759-1836). Infinite Consolation.

Charles Simeon, a notable evangelical, came to Christ when he realized it was either do that or be a hypocrite at the communion table. He became a valiant voice for faith at

Cambridge, but was locked out of his church by some of his own congregation who despised his views. Over the course of many years, his faithful presentation of the Gospel won many Cambridge men to Christ and gradually deflated his opposition.

ON HIS DEATH bed, Charles Simeon looked at those attending him. "Do you know what text greatly comforts me just now?"

"What?"

"I find infinite consolation in the fact that 'in the beginning God created the heaven and the earth!'"

This verse did not seem particularly helpful for a dying man, so they asked him what made it so to him.

"Why," he answered with a smile, "If, out of nothing, God can bring all the wonder of the world, He may yet make something out of me!"

- Adapted from F. W. Boreham's *Cliffs of Opal*. London: Epworth Press, 1948.

Sixtus V (1521-1590). A Bible full of Errors.

From lowly origins, Sixtus became pope, and was a great builder. He considered himself a great scholar.

OF ALL LITERARY BLUNDERS, none equaled that of the edition of the *Vulgate*, by Sixtus V. His Holiness carefully superintended every sheet as it passed through the press; and, to the amazement of the world, the work remained without a rival—it swarmed with errata! A multitude of scraps were printed to paste over the erroneous passages, in order to give the true text. The book makes a whimsical appearance with these patches; and the "heretics" exulted in this demonstration of papal infallibility! The copies were called in, and violent attempts made to suppress it. The world was highly amused at the bull of the editorial Pope prefixed to the first volume, which excommunicates all printers who in reprinting the work should make any alteration in the text!

His successor, Clement VIII repudiated the translation and ordered another.

- Adapted from Isaac D'Israeli's *Curiosities of Literature.* London: Frederick and Warne, 1881.

Smith, Amanda (1837-1915). Prayer as Instinct; Do Not Judge.

J. M. Thoburn, Methodist Bishop of Calcutta, first met Amanda Smith at a camp meeting in the United States and was impressed with her spirit. He later worked beside her when she visited Calcutta on an evangelistic trip. Amanda, an ex-slave who had gotten saved in a cellar, firmly believed that God directed her by inner promptings throughout her subsequent life. To judge by the results—a holy life and the salvation of numerous souls on four continents—she was right. Her Autobiography *is a stirring, original and fascinating read, often featured in women's studies. The following tales are told by Bishop Thoburn in his introduction to that autobiography.*

Instinctive prayer. DURING THE SEVENTEEN YEARS that I have lived in Calcutta, I have known many famous strangers to visit the city, some of whom attracted large audiences, but I have never known anyone who could draw and hold so large an audience as Mrs. Smith.

She assisted me both in the church and in open-air meetings and never failed to display the peculiar tact for which she is remarkable.

I shall never forget one meeting which we were holding in an open square, in the very heart of the city. It was at a time of no little excitement, and some Christian preachers had been roughly handled in the same square a few evenings before. I had just spoken myself, when I noticed a great crowd of men and boys who had succeeded in breaking up a missionary's audience on the other side of the square, rushing toward us with loud cries and threatening gestures.

If left to myself I should have tried to gain the box on which the speakers stood, in order to command the crowd, but at the critical moment, our good Sister Smith knelt on the grass and began to pray. As the crowd rushed up to the spot, and saw her with her beaming face upturned to the evening sky, pouring out her soul in prayer, they became perfectly still, and stood as if transfixed to the spot! Not even a whisper disturbed the solemn silence, and when she had finished we had as orderly a service as if we had been within the four walls of a church!

Judge not. IN THOSE DAYS a well known theatrical manager, much given to popular buffoonery, wrote to me inviting me to arrange to have Mrs. Smith preach in his theater on a certain

Sunday evening. I was much surprised on receiving the letter, and taking it to her told her I did not know what it meant. Several friends, who chanced to be present, at once began to dissuade her:

"Do not go, Sister Amanda," said several, speaking at once, "the man merely wishes to have a good opportunity of seeing you, so that he can take you off in his theater. He had no good purpose in view. Do not trust yourself to him under any circumstances."

After a moment's hesitation Mrs. Smith replied in language which I shall never forget:

"I am forbidden," she said, "to judge any man. You would not wish me to judge you, and would think it wrong if any of us should judge a brother or sister in the church. What right have I to judge this man? I have no more right to judge him than if he were a Christian."

She said she would pray over it and give her decision. She did so, and decided to accept the invitation.

When Sunday evening came the theater was packed like a herring box, while hundreds were unable to gain admission. I took charge of the meeting, and after singing and prayer introduced our strange friend from America.

She spoke simply and pointedly, alluding to the kindness of the manager who had opened the doors of his theater to her, in very courteous terms, and evidently made a deep and favorable impression upon the audience. There was no laughing, and no attempt was ever made subsequently to ridicule her. As she was walking off the stage the manager said to me:

"If you want the theater for her again do not fail to let me know. I would do anything for that inspired woman."

- Bishop J. M. Thoburn "Introduction," in Smith, Amanda. *An Autobiography; the story of the Lord's dealings with Mrs. Amanda Smith, the colored evangelist...* Chicago: Meyer and Brother, 1893.

Smith, Rodney "Gypsy" (1860-1947). A Blessing.

Gypsy Smith was indeed a gypsy. Born in a tent, he never attended a day of school and seemed destined for prison when Christ made a notable world-wide evangelist of him.

IRA D. SANKEY tells the following story about Rodney Smith: When Gypsy Smith made his first visit to America, I had the pleasure of taking him for a drive in Brooklyn. While passing through Prospect Park he asked me, "Do you remember driving out from London one day to a gypsy camp at Epping Forest?" I replied that I did. "Do you remember a little gypsy boy standing by your carriage," he asked again, "and you put your hand on his head, saying that you hoped he would be a preacher?"

"Yes, I remember it well."

"I am that boy," said Gypsy Smith

Ira D. Sankey's *My Life and the Story of the Gospel Hymns.* Philadelphia: Sunday School Times, 1907.

South, Robert (1634-1716). Sleepers Wake.

Robert South was an English clergyman and controversialist in the time of Charles the Second and Queen Anne.

DR. SOUTH, A CHAPLAIN to King Charles II of England, was preaching one day before court, which was composed of the most profligate and dissipated men in the nation. In the middle of his sermon he realized that his hearers had fallen asleep. The doctor immediately stopped short, and changing his tone of voice, called out to Lord Lauderdale three times. His lordship standing up, South said with great composure, "I am sorry to interrupt your repose, but I must beg of you that you will not snore quite so loud lest you awaken his majesty."

- Adapted from Sholto and Reuben Percy. *The Percy Anecdotes*. Harper & Brothers, 1847.

Spurgeon, Charles Haddon (1834-1892). His Extraordinary Salvation Experience.

One of the greatest preachers of the nineteenth century, with thousands sitting under his preaching, the Baptist minister and author Charles Spurgeon needs little introduction. His books, such as A Treasury of David, *are still widely read.*

I WILL TELL YOU HOW I, myself, was brought to the knowledge of this truth. It may happen that the telling of that will bring some one else to Christ. It pleased God in my childhood to convince me of sin. I lived a miserable creature, finding no hope, no comfort, thinking that surely God would never save me. At last the worst came to worst—I was miserable; I could scarcely do anything. My heart was broken in pieces. Six months did I pray, prayed agonizingly with all my heart, and never had an answer. I resolved that in the town where I lived I would visit every place of worship in order to find out the way of salvation. I felt I was willing to do anything and be anything, if God would only forgive me. I set off determined to visit the chapels, and I went to all the places of worship; and though I dearly venerate the men who occupy those pulpits now, and did so then, I am bound to say that I never heard them once fully preach the Gospel. I mean by that, they preached truth, great truths, many good truths that were fitting to many of their congregation who were spiritually-minded people; but what I wanted to know was, How can I get my sins forgiven? And they never once told me that. I wanted to know how a poor sinner, under the sense of sin, might find peace with God; and when I went I heard a sermon on, "Be not deceived. God is not mocked," which cut me up worse, but did not say how I might escape.... I was something like a dog under the table, not allowed to eat the children's food. I went time after time, and I can honestly say, I don't know that I ever went without prayer to God, and I am sure there was not a more attentive listener in all the place than myself, for I panted and longed to understand how I might be saved.

At last one day—it snowed so much that I could not go to the place to which I had determined to go, and I was obliged to stop on the road, and it was a blessed stop for me—I found rather an obscure street and turned down a court and there was a little chapel. I wanted to go somewhere, but I did not know this place. It was the Primitive Methodists' chapel. I had heard of these people from many, and how they sang so loudly that they made people's heads ache; but that did not matter. I wanted to know how I might be saved, and if they made my head ache ever so hard, I did not care...the service went on, but no preacher came. At last a very thin looking man, Rev. Robert Eaglen, came into the pulpit and opened his Bible and read these words: "Look unto me and be ye saved, all ye ends of the earth." Just setting his eyes upon me as if he knew me all by heart, he said, "Young man you are in trouble." Well, I was, sure enough. Said he, "You will never get out of it unless you look to Christ." And then lifting his hands he cried out, as I think only a Primitive Methodist could do, "Look, look, look."

"It is only look," said he. I saw at once the way of salvation. Oh! how I did leap for joy at that moment... Like as when the brazen serpent was lifted up, they only looked and were healed. I had been waiting to do 50 things, but when I heard this word, "look" what a charming word it seemed to me. Oh! I looked until I could almost have looked my eyes away...

- Russell H. Conwell. *Charles Haddon Spurgeon, the World's Greatest Preacher.* Edgewood Publishing, 1892.

Stillingfleet, Edward (1635-1699). Doctor and King.

A British theologian and deeply learned (at his death he owned 10,000 books), Stillingfleet held many high positions in the church of England.

CHARLES THE SECOND once demanded of Dr. Stillingfleet, who was a preacher to the court, why he read his sermons before him, when on every other occasion his sermons were delivered extempore? The doctor answered, that overawed by so many great and noble personages, and in the presence of his sovereign, he dared not trust his powers.

"And now," said the divine, "will your majesty permit me to ask a question?"

"Certainly," said the condescending monarch.

"Why, then, does your majesty read your speeches, when it may be presumed that you can have no such reason?"

"Why, truly," said the king, "I have asked my subjects so often for money, that I am ashamed to look them in the face."

- Adapted from Sholto and Reuben Percy. *The Percy Anecdotes*. Harper & Brothers, 1847.

Stowe, Harriet Beecher (1811-1896). Dad's Approval.

The author of Uncle Tom's Cabin *cared less for the novel's success than for a single rewarding incident in childhood.*

BY AGE SIX, Harriet was reading adult books, but hated writing. That soon changed.

One of the greatest triumphs of her life came when she was twelve. She saw her father's face brighten when her essay on immortality was read anonymously. How Lyman beamed when it won first prize and he learned that it was his own daughter's. She treasured that moment of approval more than the success of any of her later works.

- Mentioned in Stowe biographies.

Sundar Singh (1889-1929). Desperate Vision.

Sundar Singh became violently angry when his mother died. He was then a young teen and attending a Christian school in India. Embittered by the loss of his loving mother, he passed through the spiritual crisis described in this excerpt and became a notable Indian evangelist, donning the yellow robe of a holy man. On several occasions Sundar Singh carried the Gospel into Tibet where he suffered greatly. On his last venture into the forbidden country, he did not return.

THE ENCOUNTER with the Christian teachers at the school had roused a latent hostility within him, which was increased by the recent suffering he had gone through owing to his mother's death. He went to extreme lengths and led a party of youths who used to make attacks on the missionaries whenever they stood up to preach in the bazaar. Sometimes these lads would throw stones and mud at the preachers, and Sundar became their ringleader.

This form of violence in action, which was alien to his nature, came to a head in the middle of December, 1903, when Sundar brought into his father's courtyard a copy of the Christian Gospels and set fire to it in public. Such a burning of a sacred religious book was an event unheard of before in the village of Rampur.

His father was bewildered and alarmed at his son's extravagant action, which seemed to be altogether unlike him and to have a touch of madness about it.

"Why," he asked his young son, "have you done such a mad thing? Surely you are mad to do a thing like that!"

The boy made no reply, for his mind was truly distraught. He was now over fifteen, and was thus rapidly approaching the age of early manhood, for this begins sooner in India than in the West. Youth is a time in which headstrong action is always a dangerous possibility. A wild resolution seemed to possess him that he would either find out the truth that was behind all this agonizing conflict, or else put an end to himself by committing suicide. Thus the inner struggle went on, unbroken and unappeased.

"Though," he wrote, "according to my own ideas at that time, I thought I had done a good deed in burning the Gospel, yet my unrest of heart increased, and for the two following days I was very miserable. On the third day, when I could bear it no longer, I got up at three in the morning and prayed that if there was a God at all He would reveal Himself to me."

What followed formed the greatest turning-point of all his life. It must be given in his own words.

"My intention was," he said, "that if I got no satisfaction, I would place my head upon the railway-line when the five o'clock train passed by and kill myself. If I got no satisfaction in this life, I thought I would get it in the next. I was praying and praying but received no answer; and I prayed for half an hour longer hoping to get peace. At 4:30 a.m. I saw something of which I had no idea previously. In the room where I was praying I saw a great light. I thought the place was on fire. I looked round, but could find nothing. The thought came to me that this might be an answer that God had sent me. Then as I prayed and looked into the light, I saw the form of Jesus Christ. It had such an appearance of glory and love! If it had been some Hindu incarnation I would have prostrated myself before it. But it was the Lord Jesus Christ, whom I had been insulting a few days before.

"I felt that a vision like this could not come out of my own imagination. I heard a voice saying in Hindustani: 'How long will you persecute me? I have come to save you; you were praying to know the right way. Why do you not take it?' So I fell at his feet and got this wonderful peace, which I could not get anywhere else. This was the joy I was wishing to get. This was heaven itself.

"When I got up, the vision had disappeared; but although the vision disappeared, the peace and joy have remained with me ever since.

"I went and told my father that I had become a Christian. He told me: 'Go and lie down and sleep. Why, only the day before yesterday you burnt the Bible; and now you say you are a Christian!'

"I said, 'Well, I have discovered now that Jesus Christ is alive, and have determined to be His follower. Today I am his disciple, and I am going to serve Him.'"

- C. F. Andrews. *Sadhu Sundar Singh; a personal memoir.* London: Hodder and Stoughton, 1934.

Sunday, Billy (1862-1935). Raiding the Larder.

Billy Sunday was famed as an American evangelist and revival leader. A spirited child, he walked out of his grandfather's house and made his own way after his grandfather tongue-lashed him for some minor infraction that was not his fault. He would later say, "Don't stop with telling your boy to do right. Show him how." Because he was a talented runner, he was invited into major league baseball where he thrilled fans with stolen bases. When he felt God's call to become an evangelist, he asked permission to break his contract. This was refused, so he began praying for a way. The Brotherhood players merged with the National League, he could be spared, and his prayer was answered. Here is an anecdote from his childhood.

AT THE GLENWOOD SCHOOL a strict rule required prompt appearance at meals, and boys who were not on hand to the dot had to miss both that meal and the next. Somehow or other Billy found it hard to obey that rule. In later years he was generally "Johnny on the spot," but in that time he had to miss a good many meals.

To miss two meals a day is not a good thing for a growing boy, and it began to show on Billy so much that it worried his brother Ed. Ed soon managed to have himself assigned to the task of cleaning the kitchen. When his work there was finished it fell upon him to lock the door. This he faithfully did, but it often happened that little Billy was locked in the kitchen. The plate he had missed at the table Ed would tuck away in some convenient corner, and in spite of his tardiness Billy waxed fat and strong, and soon began to have a countenance as ruddy as David when he stood before Samuel.

- Elijah P. Brown. *The Real Billy Sunday; the Life and Work of Rev. William Ashley Sunday, D.D. The Baseball Evangelist.* Dayton, Ohio: Otterbein Press, 1914.

Tanner, John (died ca. 1813). Shot for Performing a Baptism.

We know little of John Tanner's early life. Born in Virginia, he became a Baptist minister sometime before 1777. Baptists were much persecuted in the early days of the United States as his story shows.

MRS. DAWSON of Windsor, North Carolina, had become a Christian and believed she should be baptized. She asked to join the church at Cashie, under Elder Dargan. Her husband violently opposed this step and threatened that if any man baptized his wife, he would shoot him, and so the baptism was put off. Eventually, when John Tanner was present, Mrs. Dawson asked again for baptism. Her confession being accepted, Elder Dargan, who was infirm, and always had others conduct his baptisms for him, asked Tanner to perform the ceremony. Whether he was told of the husband's threat or not, we do not know. At any rate, Tanner baptized Mrs. Dawson.

The following June, 1777, John Tanner was scheduled to speak at the Sandy Run meeting house. Learning of this, Mr. Dawson lay in wait for the pastor along the banks of the Roanoke River about three miles from the church. When John Tanner and Elder Dargan ascended the bank from Norfleet Ferry landing, the bitter husband shot Tanner with a large pistol and seventeen shot penetrated his thigh, one passing completely through and lodging in the other leg.

A doctor removed as much of the shot as he could, but Tanner's life was despaired of for several weeks. When he recovered, Tanner did not press charges, chalking up the event as persecution for Christ's sake.

- Adapted from Lemuel Burkitt and Jesse Read. *A Concise History of the Kehukee Baptist Association; from Its original rise down to 1808.* Lawrence, Tennessee: Henry L. Burkitt, 1850; and Roberts S. Duncan's *A History of the Baptists in Missouri,* 1882; also mentioned in Reuben Herring's *The Baptist Almanac and Repository of Indispensable Knowledge.* Nashville, Tennessee: Broadman Press, 1976.

Taylor, Edward (1793-1871). None of that Nonsense! A Question for Voltaire.

Father Taylor was a Methodist itinerant preacher who eventually found himself in Boston where his work among seamen resulted in revival.

None of that nonsense. AT THE PRAYER-MEETINGS Father Taylor cast off all restraint, and unveiled his inner nature like a child. One of his most remarkable displays of this kind was after an address by a visitor, who related the death of a very wicked man, who was blown up a few days before in a powder mill at Wilmington. He came down crushed and mangled, and gave his heart to God; and now who would not say with the holy man of old, "Let me die the death of the righteous, and let my last end be like his?" (Numbers 23:10).

Father Taylor rose at once. "I don't want any trash brought unto this altar. I hope none of my people calculate on serving the devil all their lives and cheating him with their dying breath. Don't look forward to honoring God by giving him the last snuff of an expiring candle. Perhaps you never will be blown up in a powder-mill."

"That 'holy man,'" he continued, "that we heard of was Balaam, the meanest scoundrel mentioned in the Old Testament or the New. And now I hope we shall never hear anything more from Balaam, nor from his ass."

- From Charles Spurgeon's *Eccentric Preachers*. London: Passmore and Alabaster, 1879.

A question for Voltaire. FATHER TAYLOR once preached on the text "The wicked shall be turned into hell," and began with these words, "God said that. How many piping pettifoggers of Satan will you set against his word?

"Voltaire," he exclaimed, leaning forward and looking down—"Voltaire, what do you think about it now?"

- Adapted from Walter Baxendale's *Dictionary of Anecdote, Incident, Illustrative Fact*. New York: Thomas Whittaker, 1889.

Telemachus (died ca. 400). The End of Gladiatorial Contests.

The incident below is all that we know of the monk St. Telemachus.

HONORIUS, who inherited the empire of Europe, put a stop to the gladiatorial combats which had long been held at Rome. The occasion of his doing so arose from the following circumstance. A certain man of the name of Telemachus had embraced the ascetic life. He had set out from the East and for this reason had repaired to Rome. There, when the abominable spectacle was being exhibited, he went into the stadium, and, stepping down into the arena, endeavored to stop the men who were wielding their weapons against one another. The spectators of the slaughter were indignant, and inspired by the mad fury of the demon who delights in those bloody deeds, stoned the peacemaker to death.

When the admirable emperor was informed of this, he numbered Telemachus in the array of victorious martyrs, and put an end to that impious spectacle.

- *Theodoret, Jerome, Gennadius, & Rufinus: Historical Writings.* Edited by Philip Schaff. In a Select Library of the Nicene and Post-Nicene Fathers of the Christian Church. New York: Christian Literature Publishing Co., 1892.

Ten Boom, Corrie (1892-1983). Encounter with the Indian Who Saw Christ.

Corrie Ten Boom is famous for hiding Jews from the Nazis. The movie The Hiding Place *was made from experiences recounted in her book of the same name. Another book,* In My Father's House *tells of her encounter with the most Christ-like man she ever met, the Indian mystic and evangelist Sundar Singh.*

CORRIE WAS IN HER LATE TEENS when Sadhu Sundar Singh visited the Netherlands. She had heard a great deal about this mystic who began by hating Christians and even burning a Bible, but was converted in an astonishing vision of the risen Christ. Determined to see him, but afraid there would be no room left at the conference grounds, she took her sleeping bag with her, intending to lie out in the field if necessary. A kindly worker found a place for her and she listened thrilled as Sundar Singh spoke. However, his description of his vision left her troubled. Why hadn't she experienced anything like that in her Christian life?

As she was walking in the field pondering this question, she almost ran into the Sadhu. She screwed up the courage to ask him a few questions and he put her at her ease at once and answered them.

Why hadn't she ever seen a vision or experienced a miracle? Sundar Singh smiled at her. He told her that people sometimes came to him to see a miracle. However, he would now send them to her to see a greater miracle. After all, he believed in Jesus because he had seen Him with his own eyes, but she, who had never seen Jesus, believed in Him through the testimony of the Holy Spirit.

"Don't pray for visions," he concluded. "He gives you the assurance of his presence without visions."

- Adapted from Corrie Ten Boom's *In My Father's House*. Carmel, New York: Guideposts, 1976.

Tozer, A. W. (1897-1963). Did the Doctors Tell Me Everything?

Tozer, was perhaps the most famous Christian and Missionary Alliance pastor, apart from its founder, A. B. Simpson.

FEARFUL OF GERMS, Tozer had a strong aversion to being with crowds of people, or shaking hands. He conducted hospital visitation only in the most serious cases. One story, which may be apocryphal, says that on a return from a flight he stopped at a hospital to visit one of his elders who was recovering from minor surgery. The elder turned white. "I'm not that sick, am I?" he asked. He turned to his wife, "Honey, are you sure the doctors told me everything?"

- Retold from James L. Snyder's *In Pursuit of God, the life of A.W. Tozer.* Camp Hill, Pennsylvania: Christian Publications, 1991.

Tyng, Dudley (1829-1858). Dying Words Evoked Famous Hymn.

Dudley Tyng was an energetic Episcopalian pastor and evangelist in the Philadelphia area.

DUDLEY TYNG was deeply burdened for the salvation of men. On Tuesday, March 30, 1858, he spoke to a noon rally that drew 5,000 to Jaynes' Hall in Philadelphia. He took as his text Exodus 10:11, "Go now ye that are men and serve the Lord." He declared that he would rather lose his right arm than fail to deliver God's message to his listeners. Deeply moved, 1,000 men responded to the solemn words of the young Episcopal minister.

That was his last sermon. A few days later, while patting a mule which was shelling corn in a barn, his sleeve caught in a cog and his arm was ripped off at the root with much loss of blood. Infection developed, and on April 19th, he died. His last words were, "Stand up for Jesus, father, and tell my brethren of the ministry to stand up for Jesus."

This dying exhortation inspired George Duffield to preach a memorial sermon taking as his text Ephesians 6:14: "Stand, therefore, having your loins girt about with truth, and having on the breastplate of righteousness." Duffield closed his sermon with some verses he had written. Those live on as the beloved hymn "Stand Up, Stand Up for Jesus."

- Mentioned in several books of hymn stories.

Urthazanes (Fourth Century). Broken by a Frown.

Simeon (Shem'on) was martyred about 340 under King Shapour II.

URTHAZANES, a Persian courtier, who apostatized from the Christian faith, saw Simeon, a holy bishop, led past him to martyrdom, and saluted him as he passed, but the bishop frowned upon him. Urthazanes' heart was broken, and he cried, "Ah! how shall I appear before the great God of heaven, whom I have denied, when Simeon, but a man will not endure to look upon me? If he frown, how will God behold me when l stand before His tribunal!" This led to his reclamation, and he afterwards died a martyr.

- Walter Baxendale's *Dictionary of Anecdote, Incident, Illustrative Fact.* New York: Thomas Whittaker, 1889.

Ussher, James (1581-1656). Eleventh Command.

James Ussher, a bishop of the Church of England, was famed for his calculation of the date of creation. Samuel Rutherford, a staunch and persecuted Presbyterian pastor, is noted for his deep pastoral letters and writings on governmental theory.

THERE IS A TRADITION that Archbishop James Ussher, passing through Galloway, turned aside on a Saturday to enjoy the congenial society of Samuel Rutherford. He came, however, in disguise; and, being welcomed as a guest, took his place with the rest of the family when they were catechized, as was usual, that evening. The stranger was asked, How many commandments are there? His reply was, eleven. The pastor corrected him, but the stranger maintained his position, quoting our Lord's words, "A new commandment I give unto you, that ye love one another."

They retired to rest, all interested in the stranger. Sunday morning dawned. Rutherford arose and repaired as was his custom, for meditation, to a walk that bordered on a thicket, but was startled by hearing the voice of prayer—prayer, too, for the host, and on behalf of the souls that would assemble that day. It was none other than the holy archbishop, and soon they came to an explanation. With great mutual love they conversed together, and at the request of Rutherford, the archbishop went up to the pulpit, conducted the service for the Presbyterian pastor, and preached on "The New Commandment."

- Adapted from Walter Baxendale's *Dictionary of Anecdote, Incident, Illustrative Fact*. New York: Thomas Whittaker, 1889.

Villecerf, Madame de (Undated Episode). Faith and Forgiveness.

I have been unable to find any information on Madame de Villecerf beyond this anecdote.

MADAME DE VILLECERF, who was brought to death in the flower of her age by her surgeon's lack of skill, comforted him with these words: "I do not look upon you," she said, in dying, "as a person whose error has cost me my life, but as a benefactor, who hastens my entry into a happy immortality. As the world may judge otherwise, I have put you in a situation, by my will, to quit your profession."

- *The Book of Three Hundred Anecdotes Historical, Literary, and Humorous—A New Selection.* London and New York: Burns & Oates, n.d.

Waldo, Peter (ca 1175). His Wife's Intervention.

When Waldo fell under conviction for his sins, he began his reformation by repaying those he had cheated and giving alms to the poor. Later he gave his lands to his wife, placed his daughters in a convent and reduced himself to beggary. The established church neglected God's word in those days. Waldo paid a priest to make a French translation, and using it he went among the people preaching. His reform movement was persecuted terribly by the Roman church.

ONE DAY, shortly after he had given away the last of his money, upon coming from church, he asked a citizen, once his comrade, to give him something to eat for God's sake. Leading him to his house, his friend said, "I will give you whatever you need as long as I live." When this came to the ears of his wife, she was not a little upset, and as though she had lost her mind, she ran to the archbishop of the city and implored him not to let her husband beg bread from anyone but her. This moved to tears all who were present.

Waldo was conducted into the presence of the archbishop. His wife, seizing him by the throat, said, "Is it not better, husband, that I should redeem my sins by giving you alms than that strangers should do so?" And from that time he was not allowed to take food from anyone in that city except from his wife.

- Adapted from an anonymous chronicle written early in the thirteenth century; translated by J. H. Robinson in *Readings in European History*. Boston: Ginn, 1905.

Wallace, Lew (1827-1925). An Agnostic's Rant Prompts Ben Hur.

Lew Wallace was a Union general in the Civil War. At Monocacy, he held Early's larger force at bay long enough for Washington, D.C. to mount a defense. After the war, he governed lawless New Mexico, where he wrote the historical novel Ben Hur.

SINCE CHILDHOOD Lew Wallace had been fascinated with the story of the wise men mentioned in Matthew. After attempting to turn it into fiction, he laid it aside. One day the notorious agnostic Robert Ingersoll hailed Lew Wallace as they were boarding a train. He invited Lew into his compartment where he proceeded to excoriate Christian beliefs.

Said Lew afterward, "He was in prime mood; and beginning, his ideas turned to speech, slowing like a heated river. His manner of putting things was marvelous; and ...I sat spellbound, listening to a medley of argument, eloquence, wit, satire, audacity, irreverence, poetry, brilliant antitheses, and pungent excoriation of believers in God, Christ, and Heaven, the like of which I had never heard. He surpassed himself, and that is saying a great deal.

"The speech was brought to an end by our arrival at the Indianapolis Central Station nearly two hours after its commencement. Upon alighting from the car, we separated, he to go to a hotel, and I to my brother's, a long way up northeast of town. The street-cars were at my service, but I preferred to walk, for I was in a confusion of mind not unlike dazement.

"To explain this, it is necessary now to confess that my attitude with respect to religion had been one of absolute indifference. I had heard it argued times innumerable, always without interest. So, too, I had read the sermons of great preachers...but always for the surpassing charm of their rhetoric. But—how strange! To lift me out of my indifference, one would think only strong affirmations of things regarded holiest would do. Yet here was I now moved as never before, and by what? The most outright denials of all human knowledge of God, Christ, Heaven, and the Hereafter which figures so in the hope and faith of the believing everywhere. Was the Colonel right? What had I on which to answer yes or no? He had made me ashamed of my ignorance: and then—here is the unexpected of the affair—as I walked on in the cool darkness, I was aroused for the first time in my life to the importance of religion. To write all my reflections would require many pages. I pass them to say simply that I resolved to study the subject....

"It only remains to say that I did as resolved, with results—first, the book *Ben Hur,* [which picks up the story of the three wise men] and second, a conviction amounting to absolute belief in God and the Divinity of Christ.

- Lew Wallace. *Preface to The First Christmas* (a reprint of the story of the wise men excerpted from Ben Hur). New York: Harper and Brothers, 1902.

Wardlaw, Henry (died 1440). Boundless Generosity.

Henry Wardlaw was bishop of St. Andrews from 1404-1440. During that time, he had dubious distinction of being the first to burn a martyr in Scotland—Paul Craw (Pavel Kravar), a Bohemian visitor with Hussite views, who had distributed copies of Wycliffe's Bible translation. The following anecdote shows him in a better light.

HENRY WARDLAW, bishop of St. Andrew's, at the beginning of the fifteenth-century was a prelate of such unbounded liberality, that the masters of his household, apprehensive that his revenues might be exhausted by the expense of entertaining the great numbers who resorted to his palace, solicited him to make out a list of persons to whom the hospitality of his board might be confined. "Well," said the archbishop to his secretary, "take a pen and begin. First put down Fife and Angus"—two large counties, containing several hundred thousands of people. His servants hearing this, retired abashed; "for," says the historian, "they said he would have no man refused that came to his house."

- *The Book of Three Hundred Anecdotes Historical, Literary, and Humorous—A New Selection*. London and New York: Burns & Oates, n.d.

Watts, Isaac (1674-1748). Childhood Rhymes.

Isaac Watts, an eminent dissenting minister and hymn writer, was born at Southampton in the year 1674, of parents who were distinguished by their piety and virtue. He possessed uncommon genius, and gave early, although annoying proofs of it, as this anecdote shows. Having received a good education, he made the most of his opportunities. After serious deliberation, he decided to devote his life to the ministry, and labored diligently to promote the instruction and happiness of the people under his care. By his Christian conduct and amiable disposition, he greatly endeared himself to them. Broken in health, he died with great fortitude.

WATTS WAS BROUGHT up in the home of a committed Nonconformist (one who refused to conform to Church of England practices), a man who went to prison twice rather than renege on his beliefs. He displayed a propensity for rhyming, even as a small boy, speaking so frequently in verse that it caused his parents much annoyance. His father ordered him to stop, but the rhyming persisted. Once the father started to whip him, and little Isaac is said to have cried out:

> O father, do some pity take
> And I will no more verses make.

- Many sources mention this and Watt's other childhood verses.

Wayland, Francis (1796-1865). A Soft Answer.

Dr. Francis Wayland was a Baptist minister, and for eighteen years president of Brown College; a man of deep faith who lived a singularly useful and beloved life.

DEACON MOSES POND went to Dr. Wayland once with the complaint that his preaching did not edify him. "I'm sorry," said the pastor; "I know that they are poor sermons. I wish I could make them better. Come, let us pray that I may be able to do so."

The deacon, telling the story, used to say, "Dr. Wayland prayed and I prayed; he cried and I cried. But I have thought a hundred times that it was strange that he did not turn me out of his house. I tell you, there never was a better man nor a greater preacher than Dr. Wayland."

- Adapted from Walter Baxendale's *Dictionary of Anecdote, Incident, Illustrative Fact*. New York: Thomas Whittaker, 1889.

Weaver, Jonathan (1824-1901). Resists Ignorant Opposition; Encourages Cheerful Thanksgiving.

Jonathan Weaver was a circuit rider on the western frontier of the United States with the United Brethren in Christ and an educator and bishop for many years. When he became a preacher, he had received just four months of formal education in a school with a teacher who knew hardly more than the pupils. But Jonathan learned to read, and educated himself by careful perusal of books and deep reflection. He was a strong advocate of an educated ministry, but met powerful resistance among the frontier clergy and laymen, who were deeply suspicious of learned men whom they saw as twisters of the truth. Weaver mustered every argument he could find to show the need of educated men to answer skeptics, prepare theological statements, and interpret the Bible. The first anecdote reveals the opposition he faced when he sought support for a college; the second shows the geniality of character which made him able to endure the opposition and hardships which characterized his years.

Ignorant opposition. THERE WAS A MAN named John Eckert, who, before coming to this country, had been jailed in Germany for preaching experiential religion. He was a man of good life, but of limited information. He preached a sermon from Revelation 9:2,3, in which he interpreted the smoke and locusts coming out of the pit as the college; the bottomless pit was the indefinite amount of learning—no limit to it; the smoke was the mystifying effect of human teaching; the college men, who always made everything dark about them were the locusts....John's exegesis was not in keeping with the strictest rules of logic, but it illustrated the spirit of the time. Many others thought what he said.

Geniality. WEAVER ATTENDED a holiness camp-meeting at Warsaw, Indiana, and, one day, was asked to preach to an audience of three or four hundred people. Says an eye-witness: "It was one of his ablest efforts. Saints rejoiced and gave God the glory. Dr. Foot, of New York, a great man of God, was so overcome with emotion that he could not speak for a time. Finally he exclaimed, 'Blessed man! I would love to put my arms around him.'

Bishop Weaver, overhearing this, arose and said, 'Doctor, I will help you,' and there these two men stood embracing each other, weeping like children."

Said Dr. Foot later, "I have met but few divines in America so simple, yet so profound."

- Both episodes are from Rev. A. H. Thompson's B*iography of Jonathan Weaver, D.D., a bishop in the Church of the United Brethren in Christ for thirty-five years.* Dayton, Ohio: United Brethren Publishing House, 1901.

Webster-Smith, Irene (1888-1971). Mountain Moved.

Irene Webster-Smith was an Irish missionary to Japan. So great was her dedication, that she gave up marriage to the man she loved, who felt called of the Lord to work in America. When she finally was in a position to marry, she learned he had died. Irene's life was one of triumphant faith and miracles. Here is one.

A BOY NAMED DAISHERO was dying of a contagious disease, probably tuberculosis. Irene wanted him to be near his widowed mother but had to protect her orphans, so she outfitted a rickshaw shed for the child and his mother. Behind the shed was a high mound of dirt which cut off sunlight from the window. She wished it could be removed.

Her orphans decided to do so themselves, carrying it spadefull by spadefull across the road to the beach. The work proved painfully slow, and the doctor refused to release Daishero into Irene's care unless he could have the sunshine.

Irene had to leave for three weeks on mission business. Before she left, the discouraged children took their Scripture lessons to heart and prayed that God would move the "mountain."

In her third week of absence, the children sent Irene a card, urging her to return as quickly as possible. They had a big surprise for her. When she got home they covered her eyes so that she could not see what the surprise was until they were ready. The "mountain" was gone.

Coolies had made several runs with a truck and hauled the dirt away for a fill on a playground project. The prayer of faith had been answered and Daishero could come live beside his mother while receiving sunshine.

- Retold from Russell T. Hitt's *Sensei; the Life Story of Irene Webster-Smith*. New York: Harper and Row, 1965.

Wesley, Charles (1707-1788). What Is Really Important.

Charles Wesley, as good a preacher as John, was his close associate in the work of the Methodist movement. He was also one of the ablest hymn writers of the Christian church.

IN EARLY LIFE Charles Wesley refused to be a heir to a large estate. Few would refuse such a "living" or fortune. "I have before me," said his friend Henry Moore, "the strongest testimony that can be given at this day, that he refused a living of five hundred pounds a year, choosing to remain among the people that he loved. He also refused a large fortune offered him by a lady whose relatives had quarreled with her, telling her in his usual short way, "It is unjust." The lady, after trying in vain to bend his spirit, informed him that she had struck his name out of her will, but that, nevertheless, her family should not possess the fortune. Mr. Wesley was advised to accept the fortune and give it to the relatives himself. He replied, "That is a trick of the devil; but it won't do. I know what I am now, but I do not know what I should be if I were thus made rich."

- J. B. Wakelet. *Anecdotes of the Wesleys; Illustrative of Their Character and Personal History.* New York: Carlton & Lanahan; Cincinnati: Hitchcock & Walden, 1869.

Wesley, John (1703-1791). A Heart Strangely Warmed; A Tactful Reproof.

Famed as the principle founder of Methodism, John Wesley kept a journal most of his life in which he recounted many fascinating incidents. The incident which changed his flailing efforts into effective ones took place on Wednesday, May 24, 1738. Here is what he described in his journal.

A heart strangely warmed. I THINK IT WAS about five this morning that I opened my Testament on these words, "There is given unto us exceeding great and precious promises, even that ye should be partakers of the divine nature" (2 Peter 1.4). Just as I went out, I opened again on those words, "Thou art not far from the kingdom of God." In the afternoon I was asked to go to St.

Paul's. The anthem was, "Out of the deep have I called unto thee, O Lord: Lord, hear my voice. O let your ears consider well the voice of my complaint. If thou, Lord, will be extreme to mark what is done amiss, O Lord who may abide it? For there is mercy with you; therefore shall you be feared. O Israel, trust in the Lord: for with the Lord there is mercy, and with Him is plenteous redemption. And he shall redeem Israel from all his sins."

In the evening I went very unwillingly to a society in Aldersgate-street, where one was reading Luther's *Preface to the Epistle to the Romans*. About a quarter before nine, while he was describing the change which God works in the heart through faith in Christ, I felt my heart strangely warmed. I felt I did trust in Christ, Christ alone for salvation; and an assurance was given me that He had taken away my sins, even mine, and saved me from the law of sin and death.

I began to pray with all my might for those who had in a more especial manner despitefully used me and persecuted me. I then testified openly to all there what I now first felt in my heart. But it was not long before the enemy suggested, "This cannot be faith; for where is your joy?" Then was I taught that peace and victory over sin are essential to faith in the Captain of our salvation; but that, as to the transports of joy that usually attend the beginning of it, especially in those who have mourned deeply, God sometimes gives, sometimes withholds them, according to the counsels of his own will.

After I returned home, I was much buffeted with temptations; but cried out, and they fled away. They returned again and again. I as often lifted up my eyes and He "sent me help from his holy place." And herein I found the difference between this and my former state chiefly consisted. I was striving, yea, fighting with all my might under the law, as well as under grace. But then I was sometimes, if not often, conquered; now, I was always conqueror.

• John Wesley. *The Journal of John Wesley.*

A tactful reproof. ON ONE OCCASION when John Wesley was traveling, he had for a fellow-passenger in the coach an officer who was intelligent, and very agreeable in conversation; but there was one very serious drawback—his profanity. When they changed coaches Mr. Wesley took the officer aside, and after expressing the pleasure he had enjoyed in his company, said he had a great favor to ask of him. The young officer said, "I will take great pleasure in obliging you, for I am sure you will not make an unreasonable request."

"Then," said Mr. Wesley, "as we have to travel together some distance, I beg if I should so far forget myself as to swear, you will kindly reprove me."

The officer immediately saw the motive and felt the force of the request, and, smiling, said, "None but Mr. Wesley could have conceived a reproof in such a manner." The reproof acted like a charm.

• J. B. Wakelet. *Anecdotes of the Wesleys; Illustrative of Their Character and Personal History.* New York: Carlton & Lanahan; Cincinnati: Hitchcock & Walden, 1869.

Wesley, Samuel (1662-1735). The Burning of His Rectory; A Curate with a One-Track Mind.

Samuel Wesley, the father of John and Charles Wesley, along with seventeen other children, and the husband of the gifted

Susannah Wesley, was rector of Epworth. He did not evidence a particularly mature Christian character and became so embroiled in politics as to bring persecution upon himself and create distance in his relations with his wife.

Rectory burned. THE ELECTION FOR THE COUNTY of Lincoln in May, 1705, was very bitter and exciting. Mr. Samuel Wesley, with more valor than discretion, entered warmly into the contest in support of the candidate of the Orangemen, who was, nevertheless, defeated; and, on his return from the polling-place at the county-seat, the Epworth Jacobites celebrated their victory by raising a mob, which surrounded the rectory and kept up a din of drums, shouts, noise of firearms, and such like, till after midnight.

The next evening one of the mob, passing the yard where the rector's children were playing, cried out, "O you devils! we will come and turn you all out of doors a-begging, shortly;" a threat which must have had a strange significance to the Wesleys, whose fathers had suffered that identical outrage at the hands of the Church to which the rector was now devoting his tongue and his pen. It would have been "an eye for an eye" if the Jacobites had been able to execute their threat by means of another revolution; but as they were not they kept up an infamous style of persecution, stabbing the rector's cows, cutting off a leg of his dog, withholding his tithes, arresting and thrusting him into jail for small debts, and finally, after one or two unsuccessful attempts, burning the rectory to the ground, and fulfilling their threat of turning him and his family out of doors.

This last event occurred when his son John was about six years old. In the dead of a winter's night the father was awakened by the fire coming into his chamber through the thatched roof, and, hastily arousing his family, they fled down stairs, and with great difficulty escaped with their lives. By mischance little John was left behind, fast asleep; but awakening, he sprang to the window and began to cry for help. The frantic father tried in vain to ascend the stairs, but they were already too far gone to support his weight; and, half dead with suffocation and frantic with distress, he fell on his knees and commended his poor lost boy to God. Meanwhile a stout man had placed himself against the house, and another had climbed upon his shoulders, and little Jack, leaping into his arms, was rescued out of the very jaws of flame. The next instant the whole blazing mass of the roof fell in...

John Wesley was always deeply affected by this narrow escape from such a terrible death, and on the margin of a picture which was painted to commemorate the event, he wrote the significant words: "Is this not a brand plucked from the burning?"

- W. H. Daniels. *The Illustrated History of Methodism in Great Britain and America; from the days of the Wesleys to the present time.* New York: Philips and Hunt, 1880.

A Curate with a one-track mind. SAMUEL WESLEY had a curate who preached in his absence. The curate had, probably, some time in his life, lost a sixpence or so by some insolvent debtor, which made him very cautious. For a while he would preach on nothing but paying debts. Complaint being made to the rector that the curate had wearied the people with his repeated homilies on this subject, Mr. Wesley requested him one day to preach on faith, giving him for the text, "Without faith it is impossible to please God." So, after taking a week to write his sermon, the curate began, "Faith, my hearers, produces many good effects. Among others, it makes us pay our debts as soon as we can."

- George Coles. *Heroines of Methodism.* New York: Carlton & Lanahan, 1869.

Whately, Richard (1787-1863). A Spirited Pun.

Richard Whately, Archbishop of Dublin, was celebrated for his wit. Here is an example.

WHATELY ONCE STARTLED his listeners by asking "If the devil lost his tail, where would he go to find a new one?" And without waiting for others to guess, replied, "To a gin palace, for bad spirits are retailed there."

- W. Davenport Adams. *Modern Anecdotes; a treasury of wise and witty sayings of the last hundred years.* London, Hamilton, Adams, 1886.

White, Paul (1910-1992). Asthma; Canadian Wetting.

Paul White, an Australian physician better known as "Jungle Doctor" served as a missionary doctor to Africa and, through his animal fables and radio broadcasts, as an evangelist to the world.

Asthma. PAUL WHITE SUFFERED asthma severe enough to have sidelined many people. As a youngster, his mother required him to cut a hedge which triggered his breathing problems. She assumed his symptoms were faked to get out of the job, so he always had to finish. Later as a doctor in Africa, he suffered so greatly from this ailment that at times he had to be pushed to his hospital duties in a wheelbarrow! Back in Australia he was in the hospital one night on oxygen because of the same problem. His nurse inquired if he were a Christian. When he replied in the affirmative, she asked him to explain to her how she might become one herself. Paul was having so much difficulty breathing he asked if she could wait until the next day. Her answer was not particularly reassuring. "I'd rather you told me tonight," she said, "because you are on the critical list." Between gasps, Paul managed to tell her how to be saved. Perhaps he was the more willing to do so when he remembered the many times he had asked the same question as a child and been brushed off without a satisfactory answer.

Canada wetting. WHILE PAUL was visiting in Canada, he stayed as a guest in a private home. He was deep in conversation with his host and another man when his host's five year old daughter walked down stairs stark naked with a dripping nightgown under her arm. The girl pointed a finger at each of them in turn: "You or you or you didn't put the lid down and I fell in."

- Both stories are retold from Paul White's autobiography *Alias Jungle Doctor*. Paternoster Press, 1977.

Whitefield, George (1714-1770). A Humble Reply; Concern for Perchers; Dying Words.

The notable evangelists George Whitefield and John Wesley were at one time associates in seeking holiness, but their Calvinist-Arminian differences later separated them. Both remained active soul-winners to the last.

A humble reply. A minister was in company with Mr. Whitefield, and during the interview was very free with reflections on Wesley and his followers. Finally he expressed a doubt concerning Mr. Wesley's salvation, and said to George Whitefield, "Sir, do you think when we get to heaven we shall see John Wesley?"

"No, Sir," replied Whitefield, "I fear not; for he will be so near the eternal throne, and we shall be at such a distance, we shall hardly get a sight of him."

- J. B. Wakelet. *Anecdotes of the Wesleys; Illustrative of Their Character and Personal History.* New York: Carlton & Lanahan; Cincinnati: Hitchcock & Walden, 1869.

Concern for perchers. The parsonage at Cneter Groton was the scene of one of the most remarkable sermons of this great preacher [Whitefield]. The upper windows of the house were removed and a platform raised in front, facing a large yard full of forest trees. When Whitefield passed through the window to this stand and cast his eye over the multitude, he saw a number of young men, who, imitating Zaccheus in the sycamore, had climbed these trees and were perched on their limbs. The kind-hearted orator asked them to come down, saying, "Sometimes the power of God falls on these occasions and takes away the might of young men. I wish to benefit your souls and not have your bodies fall out of these trees. He literally expected to see them, under the power of the Spirit, fall down to the ground as birds that were shot; and choosing the valor of discretion they came down, only to be prostrated under the sermon. Great numbers of his hearers went home to lead new lives, and it is said that more than one of these young men became preachers of the Methodist faith.

- Adapted from Thomas Armitage's *A History of the Baptists traced by their Vital Principles and Practices from the Time of Our Lord and Savior Jesus Christ to the Year 1886.* New York: Bryan, Taylor & Co., 1887.

Dying words. On a beautiful Saturday in the latter part of September, Whitefield rode from Portsmouth to Exeter, where he was expected, and preached to a great multitude already assembled in the fields beneath a rich autumnal sky, and surrounded by the golden harvest. Before he went out, someone remarked he was more fit to go to bed than to preach.

"True, sir," replied the dying man, who turned aside, and clasping his hands ejaculated, "Lord Jesus, I am weary in thy work, but not of it. If I have not yet finished my course, let me go and speak for you once more in the field, seal your truth, and come home to die;" and it seemed like prophetic prayer: once more he went forth, and the forests rang with the melody of his tones, and men hung on his words as if they had been the words of an angel.

He rode on to Newburyport, and again spoke a few words that evening from the steps of the house where he stayed. His servant, seeing how ill he was, said he wished he would not preach so much. To this Whitefield replied, "I had rather wear out than rust out." He then prayed that God would bless the preaching he had done that day and that he hoped to do the following day. There were to be no more sermons, however; near morning he died.

- Adapted from Helen C. Knight's *Lady Huntington and Her Friends.* New York: American Tract Society, 1853 and other accounts.

Wilberforce, William (1759-1833). Love of Books; Daily Refreshment; Personal Danger.

William Wilberforce was a statesman and philanthropist, a staunch opponent of slavery, which he helped abolish, becoming one of the greatest benefactors the world has ever known.

Love of books. IN HIS RECOLLECTIONS of Wilberforce, John S. Harford tells that when Wilberforce traveled he carried books stuffed into all his pockets, as well as a green bagfull in a corner of the carriage. He pulled them out with delight and could find his way almost instantly to passages he desired to share. According to others, this love of books of all varieties, from Latin and Greek classics to sermons, lasted with him all his life. He memorized large passages and heavily annotated the margins of many, dialoging with the authors, as it were.

Times of refreshing. ONE SECRET of Wilberforce's strength and staying power, was the time he set apart for the Lord. Each day he allotted an hour to devotions, usually in the morning. He kept every Sunday free of work, attending church, or hearing sermons or listening to devotional books read aloud, thus refreshing his heart and his frail frame. He also loved to walk in gardens, to pick flowers, and to listen to birds sing. Listening once to Handel's *Messiah,* he burst into tears at the "Hallelujah Chorus." All of this was beneficial to his health, for he sometimes suffered such severe intestinal pain that he had to take opium for relief.

Personal danger. In his fight to abolish slavery, Wilberforce exposed the character of some slave traders, among whom was Captain John Kimber. Through the connivance of the court, Kimber was cleared of the charges against him and demanded Wilberforce apologize and pay him a huge indemnity. Wilberforce refused, whereupon for two years he found it necessary to travel with someone to protect him, for Kimber vowed to retaliate with violence, and laid in wait for him on several occasions.

- All of these anecdotes are retold from Kevin Belmonte's *Hero for Humanity; a biography of William Wilberforce*. Colorado Springs, Colorado: NavPress, 2002.

Wilks, Matthew (1746-1829). Matchmaker.

Matthew Wilks, London preacher, was a father of The London Missionary Society, the Evangelical Magazine, *the Irish Evangelical Society, the Bible Society, and the Religious Tract Society.*

MATTHEW WILKS, a great soul-winner, was also rather eccentric. Here is how he found a wife for a brother minister. He sent him to the lady's house with this laconic note:

My dear madam,
Allow me to introduce to you my worthy friend, the Rev. Mr. A—
If you're a cat
You'll smell a rat!

Yours truly,

MATT. WILKS.

The lady found it needful to request the gentleman to explain the letter; this led them into pleasant conversation, and into mutual admiration, which ended in marriage. The mystery of the cat and the rat was thus solved.

- Adapted from Charles Spurgeon's *Eccentric Preachers*. London: Passmore and Alabaster, 1879.

Willard, Frances A (1839-1898). Emancipation.

Frances Willard was famed for her leadership of women in the fight to abolish alcoholic beverages and as an organizer of women for social causes. She became most Christ-like. It was not always so as this anecdote shows.

FRANCES WILLARD CELEBRATED the arrival of her eighteenth birthday by writing the following:

> I am eighteen.
> I have been obedient.
> Not that the yoke was heavy to be borne,
> For lighter ne'er did parents fond
> Impose on child.
> It was a silver chain,
> But the bright adjective
> Takes not away the clinking sound!
> The clock has struck!

I'm free! Come joy profound!
I'm alone and free –
Free to obey Jehovah only,
Accountable but to the powers above!

Then she took *Ivanhoe*, seated herself on the porch and began to read with calm satisfaction. Her father chanced up the steps.

"What have you there?"

"One of Scott's novels."

"Have I not forbidden you to read any novels?"

"You forget what day it is, Father."

"What difference does the day make in the deed?"

"A great deal. I am eighteen today, and I do not have to obey any laws but those of God hereafter. In my judgment, *Ivanhoe* is good to be read."

The amazed father was for half an instant minded to take away the book by force. Then he laughed, called her mother, and the two contemplated this woman-child of theirs. At length he said, seriously, "She is evidently a chip off the Puritan block." Hers was an old-fashioned Protestant declaration of independence. "Well, we will try to learn God's laws and obey them together, my child."

- From Anna A. Gordon's *The Beautiful Life of Francis Willard*. Chicago, Illinois: Women's Temperance Publishing Association, 1898.

Wilson, Walter (1881-1969). Different Reactions to His Conversion.

Walter Wilson became famed as an evangelist and doctor. He authored The Romance of a Doctor's Visits, *object lessons drawn from his medical practice.*

IN HIS BIOGRAPHY of Walter Wilson, Kenneth Gangel tells that when Walter finally understood that salvation is a free gift from God through Christ, he looked up and talked to God one evening under the stars and accepted Christ as his Savior. He felt joy and knew something had happened; just what he could not say. His two little sisters also noticed a difference the next day when he helped dress him. One ran to their mother and said "Mother, something must have happened to Walter. He didn't stick us once this morning." What amazed Walter was that he didn't even want to stick them.

A short time afterward, he shared his thrilling salvation experience with his Sunday school teacher. Works-oriented, she ordered him out of her house and refused to listen to him again.

- Derived from Kenneth O. Gangel. *Walter L. Wilson, the beloved physician.* Chicago: Moody Press, 1970.

Wordsworth, Dora (1804-1847). A Poem with Eternal Meaning.

Dora Wordsworth was the daughter of the famed English poet William Wordsworth and his wife Mary.

WHEN DORA WORDSWORTH WAS DYING, she took little interest in anything, until someone read the words of a Charlotte Elliott hymn to her. The hymn was "Just As I Am." Dora then begged to have it read to her again and again, sometimes many times a day, and seemed to draw deep comfort from the words.

> Just as I am, without one plea,
> But that Thy blood was shed for me

And that Thou biddest me come to Thee,
O Lamb of God, I come.

The author, Charlotte Elliott, had penned the words at a time when illness made her feel useless and she even felt God might have cast her aside. Before her death, she had received hundreds of letters testifying to conversions through that hymn. 43-year-old Dora Wordsworth died with hope because of those words.

- Derived from various collections of hymn stories, from Sankey's *Story of My Life and Hymns,* and from F. W. Boreham's *Late Lark Ascending.*

Writers in Prison (Various dates).

IMPRISONMENT HAS NOT ALWAYS DISTURBED the man of letters in the progress of his studies, but has unquestionably greatly promoted them.

We have, of course, several letters of Paul, which entered the New Testament, written during his imprisonment.

In prison Boethius composed his beloved work *The Consolation of Philosophy;* and Grotius wrote his *Commentary on Saint Matthew,* and other works.

Buchanan, in the dungeon of a monastery in Portugal, composed his excellent *Paraphrases of the Psalms of David. The Pilgrim's Progress* of Bunyan was created within the confines of a prison's walls. Penn's *No Cross, No Crown* was penned in prison.

Cardinal Polignac formed the design of refuting the arguments of the skeptics which Bayle had been renewing in his dictionary; but his public occupations hindered him. Two exiles at length fortunately gave him the leisure; and the *Anti-Lucretius* is the fruit of the court disgraces of its author.

In our own era, we can point to the prison letters of Dietrich Bonhoeffer and to Alexander Solzhenitsyn's massive documentary, *The Gulag Archipelago,* which did so much to bring down the Soviet empire.

- Adapted and expanded from Isaac D'Israeli's *Curiosities of Literature.* London: Frederick and Warne, 1881.

Wycliffe, John (ca. 1320-1384). Denouncing the Friars from His Sick Bed.

John Wycliffe was one of the greatest intellects of the fourteenth century. He used his knowledge to advance practical spiritual reform. Among the tasks he set himself were training preachers (the Lollards) and translating the Bible into Middle English.

THE COUNCIL WHICH CONDEMNED WYCLIFFE'S theses was composed largely of monks, several from the mendicant orders. After his disagreement with the church in doctrine, they pursued him with a flood of vituperation and with pamphlets bitter and malicious. Clerical fraternal hatred is very bitter...

Then, too, the friars were the collectors of money for Bishop Spencer's crusade against their fellow Christians of Flanders, which Wycliffe opposed as inhuman and heathenish. The expedition was a complete flop, the mendicants had to share in the opprobrium, and they hated the reformer more intensely as if he were responsible for their humiliation.

Once when he was very sick at Oxford and supposed to be at the point of death, four friars from the four leading orders...visited Wycliffe. They exhorted him strongly to recant what he had said against their orders and to be reconciled with the brotherhood. They evidently hoped for an easy victory over their weakened arch-enemy. But he called for his servant to lift him up on his pillows, and holding them with his glittering eye, with a vigor worthy of an ancestral Viking, he cried, "I shall not die but live, and again declare the evil deeds of the friars."

- George S. Innes. *Wycliffe: the morning star.* Cincinnati, Ohio: L Jennings and Graham, 1907.

Ximinez de Cisneros, Cardinal (1436-1517). Weeping for His Enemies.

As inquisitor of Spain, Ximinez was far milder than most of his predecessors and successors. His good sense was further shown by his opposition to the sale of indulgences and his funding of the first printing of a polyglot (multi-language) Bible. A man of great ability, he served as Bishop of Toledo, regent of Spain in the absence of its king, and led troops in successful battle in North Africa.

AT THE SIEGE OF ORAN, in Africa, Cardinal Ximenez led the Spanish troops to the breach, mounted on a charger, dressed in his pontifical robes, and preceded by a monk on horseback, who bore his archiepiscopal cross. "Go on, go on, my children," he exclaimed to the soldiers, "I am at your head. A priest should think it an honor to expose his life for his religion. I have an example in my predecessors, in the archbishopric of Toledo. Go on to victory."

When his victorious troops took possession of the town, he burst into tears on seeing the number of the dead that were lying on the ground; and was heard to say to himself, "They were indeed infidels, but they might have become Christians. By their death, they have deprived us of the principal advantage of the victory we have gained over them."

- *The Book of Three Hundred Anecdotes Historical, Literary, and Humorous—A New Selection.* London and New York: Burns & Oates, n.d.

Young, Rosa (1890-1971). Trusting God on 35¢.

Born a black woman in Alabama, Rosa Jinsey Young knew from childhood that she wanted to be a teacher. With heroic effort she labored to get an education for herself (schooling was not readily available to African-Americans), and then built and opened a school for black children who had known only ignorance and squalor. Every step was a struggle; she had to do the work of several people and only faith in God and desperate prayer kept her going. Finally there came a time when it seemed she could go no further. We often hear George Müller and Hudson Taylor held up as giants of prayer and perseverance. This excerpt from Rosa's autobiography shows that, although unsung, she was in their league. The Lutheran church eventually embraced her work, helping her found a chain of over 30 schools, a college and several churches in Alabama's "Dark Belt."

WHEN SCHOOL CLOSED that spring, 1915, I had only $12.85 with which to pay the salaries. I gave Sister Viola $12.50, and I kept 35 cents for my salary that year. The saddest part of all was that Sister Viola, who had been with me all through school and from the beginning in this school-work, resigned and accepted a position in the city school of Prattville, Ala., at a salary of $60 a month.

After my sister's resignation I went about in meditation and prayer, trying to make up my mind to resign and also try to secure a position in a school paying a big salary; but somehow I could not resign so easily. There was a tie between me and the little colored children of my school. I could not entertain the thought of turning them out of school, closing the doors, and letting them go back into darkness, ignorance and superstition. Such a thought was painful to me. No, I could not close the doors. Besides, I felt that by closing the school, all the donations that had been given by our kind white friends would be lost and that thereafter they would look upon us as people who start things but never finish them.

Thus, not willing to give up the school, I called together our local board of trustees. At this meeting we all agreed to offer the school to the African Methodist Episcopal Church, as we were all members of that branch of the Methodists at that time. This body was to hold an educational meeting in Selma that June (1915). I decided that it was best for me to go to Selma prior to this session, take the matter up with the president of Payne University, and get him to make the recommendation for us, as he had charge of all the educational affairs of that branch of the Methodists in Alabama at that time.

The worst of it all was that I wished to go to Selma and adjust these matters, but did not have my train-fare; I had only those 35¢.

What did I do? One Saturday evening I took those 35¢, boarded the train and went to Camden. When I arrived there, I had only ten cents left, and it was nearly sunset, as the train had been late. Where was I to lodge that night? With only a dime I could do nothing. However, I had some relatives who lived about two and a half miles out of Camden. There was nothing left for me to do but to try to reach their home. When I arrived there, they were greatly surprised to see me at that late hour, and all alone. I told them of my mission in Camden.

The next morning, Sunday, I hurried to the parsonage of the Methodist preacher. I showed him my recommendations from Mr. J. Lee Bonner, Mr. J. C. Harper, and the Hon. J. T. Dale. Then I asked the privilege of addressing his congregation in the interest of my school at Rosebud. This he readily granted me. I thanked God in my heart, for I was trying to raise my fare to Selma. Just before the minister closed his service that night, he permitted me to speak to his people. The good people of Camden gave me a nice little collection. I do not remember the amount, but among those who gave were Mr. and Mrs. Ned Allen, who are now charter members of our Lutheran mission at Camden.

That Monday morning when I returned to Neenah, I went to the post office for my mail. I received a letter from Mrs. Irving, Brooklyn on the Hudson, New York, enclosing a check for $5. I was very much uplifted in spirit, for now I had more than my fare to Selma...

- Rosa Jinsey Young. *Light in the Dark Belt*. St. Louis, Missouri: Concordia, 1929.

Index

Abbot, George 7
Adventists 97
Albert the Great 14
Alexander, Archibald 8
Alfred, King of England 9
Alphege 12
Anabaptists 170
Ancillon, David 11
Annan, Robert 11
Aquinas, Thomas 13
Argyll, Marquis of 14
Armenian Massacre 210
Arnauld, Antoine 15
Arsenius 19
Asbury, Francis 15
Askew, Anne 18
Asser 9
Athanasius 19
Augustine of Hippo 21
Aylward, Gladys 22
Bach, Johann Sebastian 23
Baltus, Pietje 151
Basil the Great 24
Baxter, Richard 27
Bede 27
Ben Hur 243
Bernard of Clairvaux 29
Berridge, John 30
"Blest be the Tie that Binds" 85
Boethius 265
Bonhoeffer, Dietrich 266
Bowles, Charles 30
Bradford, William 31
Brand, Evelyn 32
Brand, Paul 33
Bray, Billy 34
Brown, Samuel Robbins 35
Bunyan, John 36, 265
Byles, Mather 36
Calvin, John 38, 83,
Canute 40
Carey, William 41
Carmichael, Amy 42
Cartwright, Peter 43

Carver, George W. 46
"Castaway, The" 59
Chalmers, James 47
Charlemagne 49
Charles II, King of England 129, 145, 228
Charles IX, King of France 122
Chesterton, G.K. 51
Chicago Fire 216
Christmas 31
Chrysostom, John 51
Clarke, Adam 53
Clarke, Hannah 54
Columba 56
Constantine 20
Covenanters 117, 169
Cowper, William 58
Cranmer, Thomas 60, 170
Creation, The 120
Cromwell, Oliver 62
Cruden, Alexander 64
Crusaders 109
Donatists 21
Donne, John 67
Doremus, Sarah 69
Duffield, George 239
Dyneka, Peter 69
Elizabeth I, Queen of England 113
Elliot, Jim 80
Elliott, Charlotte 264
Erasmus 80, 92
Escapes 81
Eusebius of Samosata 82
Faraday, Michael 84
Farel, William 39
Fawcett, John 85
Fénelon, François 86
Finney, Charles 90
Fisher, John 92
Forsyth, Christina 93
Fox, George 94
Free Will Baptists 30, 202
French Revolution 95
Gaddis, Maxwell Pierson 97
Gardeau, Father 100
George III, King of England 102

Gilmour, James 102
Gilpin, Bernard 106
Girard, Catalan 108
Godfrey of Bouillon 109
Goodwin, Thomas 110
Gregory the Great, Pope 110
Grenfell, Wilfred 112
Grindal, Edmund 113
Grotius, Hugo 81
Ham, Mordecai 114
Handel, George Frederick 115
Harris, Samuel 116
Harvie, Marion 117
Hastings, Selina 119
Haydn, Franz Joseph 120
Haynes, Lemuel 121
Hennuyer, Jean 121
Henry VIII, King of England 61, 62, 92, 123, 152, 154
Henry, Philip 122, 168
Herbert, George 123
Hill, Rowland 126
Hooker, Richard 127
Hottentots 170
Howie, John 128
Hunt, John 129
Hyde, John 130
Ingersoll, Robert 243
Innocent IV, Pope 13
Isidore of Seville 219
Jaffray, Robert 132
James I, King of England 7, 169
Jefferson, Thomas 155
Jerome 133
Jogues, Isaac 134
"John Gilpin" 58
Jones, E. Stanley 137
Jones, Sam P. 139
Josquin des Prez 141
Jubilee Singers 206
Judson, Adoniram 142
Julian, Emperor 26
"Just as I Am" 264
Kagawa, Toyohiko 143
Kelly, John 143
Ken, Thomas 144

Ketcham, Robert T. 147
Kimbrough, Isaac B. 149
Knox, John 150
Kuyper, Abraham 151
Lassenius, John 152
Latimer, Hugh 152
Leland, John (1506-1552) 154
Leland, John (1754-1841) 155
Leprosy 33
Lewis, C.S. 155
Linley, Ozias 157
Livingstone, John 158
Loch Ness Monster 57
Lombard churches 159
Lottery 178
Louis IX, King of France 160
Louis XIV, King of France 86, 89
Louis XI, King of France 167
Louis XII of France 141
Loyalists 36
Luther, Martin 161
Maillard, Oliver 167
Man Born to Be King, the 216
Maori 218
Maillard, Oliver 167
Marshall, Daniel 167
Mary, Queen of Scots 150
Matthews, Katherine 168
McCheyne, Robert M. 165
McDowell, Josh 166
McClanahan, Anne Elizabeth 112
Melville, Andrew 169
Messiah, the 115, 260
Miller, William 97
Moffat, Robert 170
Montgomery, James 171
Moody, Dwight L. 173, 214
Morgan, G. Campbell 174
Neesima Shimeta 174
Newton, John 175
Nida, Eugene 177
Oberlin, John Frederick 179
Pain, the Gift Nobody Wants 33
Paton, John G. 184
Peck, John M. 185
Penn, William 187

Perronet, Edward 194
Peter (Apostle) 82
Peters, Hugh 195
Phillips, Wendell 196
Pike, Ken 197
Pluralties 29
Prankard, Emily 103
Prison writings 265
Pryor, Mary Bray 198
Puns 36
Radstock, Lord 198
Radzevil, Nicolas 200
Ramabai, Pandita 201
Randal, Benjamin 202
Raper, William H. 204
Roberts, Benjamin T. 205
Roberts, Robert R. 206
Robinson Crusoe 176
Robinson, Reuben 209
Rohner, Beatrice 210
Roman games 99, 236
Rufinus 133
Rutherford, Samuel 212, 241
Ryan, Patrick 213
Sang, Mansur 213
Sankey, Ira D. 214, 225
Sayers, Dorothy 221
Scudder, Ida 217
Selwyn, George 218
Seville, Council of 219
Sidney, Philip 220
Simeon, Charles 220
Sixtus V, Pope 221
Smith, Amanda 222
Smith, Rodney 225
Solzhenitsyn, Alexander 265
South, Robert 225
Spurgeon, Charles H. 226
St. Bartholomew Day Massacre 122
Stillingfleet, Edward 228
Stowe, Harriet B. 229
Sundar Singh 229, 237
Sunday, Billy 232
Tanner, John 233
Taylor, Edward 235
Telemachus 236

Ten Boom, Corrie 237
Tozer, A. W. 238
Tu, Elder 70
Tyng, Dudley 239
Ussher, James 240
Valens, Emperor 25, 82
Villecerf, Madame de 241
Voltaire 236
Waldenses 108, 242
Waldo, Peter 242
Wallace, Lew 243
Wardlaw, Henry 245
Watts, Isaac 246
Wayland, Francis 247
Weaver, Jonathan 247
Webster-Smith, Irene 249
Wesley, Charles 115, 250
Wesley, John 56, 119, 194, 251, 253, 255, 258
Wesley, Samuel 253
Whately, Richard 256
White, Paul 256
Whitefield, George 119, 258
Wilberforce, William 260
Wilks, Matthew 261
Willard, Frances 262
Wilson, Walter 264
Witter, Madeline 183
Wordsworth, Dora 264
Wycliffe, John 266
Ximinez de Cisneros 267
Young, Rosa 268

www.ingramcontent.com/pod-product-compliance
Lightning Source LLC
Chambersburg PA
CBHW031947080426
42735CB00007B/291